How To Make Money While Watching TV

**How You Can Become Financially Independent
Through Publishing In Three Easy Steps And Less
Than Six Months**

**Everything You Need To Know About How To Turn
Ideas Into Books And Books Into Money**

Vernon Coleman

BLUE
BOOKS

© Vernon Coleman 2001

The right of Vernon Coleman to be identified as the author of this work has been asserted in accordance with the Copyright, Designs and Patents Act 1988.

Parts of this book appeared under the title *How To Publish Your Own Book*.

ISBN 1 899726 30 6

With thanks to Sue Ward and the staff at Publishing House.

A catalogue record for this book is available from the British Library.

Printed and bound by J.W. Arrowsmith Limited, Bristol

CONTENTS LIST

How To Be A Publisher – Part Three   47
How To Sell Your Books

How To Be A Publisher – Part Four   99

How To Increase Your Profits (And Make Even More Money)

Afterword   114

Glossary   115

For
Donna Antoinette Coleman

A LETTER FROM THE AUTHOR

Dear Publisher-To-Be,

Yesterday, while watching an old Humphrey Bogart movie, I made £245. The day before, while whiling away a couple of hours watching snooker on television, I made £356.

Intrigued? Jealous? You don't need to be. You can do exactly the same.

Publishing is fun. It is something you can do with pride. But it is also something that you can do with profit.

For centuries publishing has been a well-established route to independence and wealth. It still is. And there's a bonus too: publishing will give you a voice in a world where most voices have been silenced. As a publisher you will have a voice and you will have influence.

Traditional book publishers, like everyone else with a trade to protect, have always done their best to make everyone think that there is some mystery about what they do.

But publishing books isn't like repairing a Ferrari engine or performing a heart by-pass operation. You don't need years of experience. And you don't need to serve a long apprenticeship alongside experienced professionals.

This book contains all the secrets you'll need to become a member of the powerful élite who influence the way people think and act.

Publishing has been, is, and always will be, a profitable business to enter because the human thirst for knowledge is literally inexhaustible.

And don't be alarmed by the computer nerds who claim that the internet will make books irrelevant and unwanted. Don't believe a word of it. They're talking absolute nonsense. The internet is a sometimes useful source of information but it is (and will be for some time) slow and difficult to use. Next time you hear a computer nerd claim that book publishers will be put out of business by the internet just remind him or her that some of the biggest and best known internet sites exist to sell books!

You Can Make Money Through Publishing

Most published authors earn such a pittance from their work that they have to do something else to earn a living. For every author who receives a million dollar advance there are thousands of authors who, after they have deducted their essential expenses, receive an hourly rate that would draw a derisory sneer from a fast-food outlet employee.

By the time bookshops and publishers have taken their cut there is very little left for the author. The traditional author's hardback contract gives an author 10% of the published price, but this percentage is often reduced (in some cases considerably) if the edition is a paperback or a low cost book club edition.

So, if books are sold in such vast numbers and most authors never see much of the money, who's making the profit?

Well, for a start there is the bookshop owner.

While most authors are lucky if they receive 10% of the published price of their book the bookshop owner and the wholesaler will between them often take half (or even more) of the published price. If you think that the bookseller's role is worth five times the role of the author then you will undoubtedly regard this as an entirely equitable state of affairs.

The bottom line is that there are far more rich booksellers and publishers in the world than there are rich authors. And many of the richest booksellers and publishers are people like you: individuals who work for themselves rather than for large international corporations.

Use the secrets in this book to help you publish a book or report (either your own or one written by someone else) and there is a good chance that you will not only be able to make a living out of doing something that you enjoy but that you will be able to build up and develop an extremely profitable business. Your big advantage will be that as publisher *and* bookseller you will receive all the profits that are normally split between publisher and bookseller! And if you write your own book or report you'll get the percentage that goes to the author too!

Start a publishing business and you can become independent and in control of your own life and destiny. Back in the early 1980s I wrote a book called *Bodypower*. It became a huge best-seller – reaching the Top Ten lists in both *The Sunday Times* and *The Bookseller*. A few years ago I bought back the rights to that book, which is now part of my self-published 'backlist'. I've made far more money out of that book as a self publisher than I made when it was an official best-seller – published by big name publishing companies.

Publishing Can Give You Independence

Your happiness on this earth depends to a very large extent upon the amount of freedom you have. It is difficult to find contentment if you are a slave. And, in our society, the amount of freedom you enjoy depends to a certain extent upon the amount of money you have. Money can buy you freedom.

I do not approve of this state of affairs. It is quite wrong. But it is how things are and it would be foolish to deny it and pointless to try to fight against it.

Clearly, therefore, making money – on your own terms – is an integral part of finding contentment. You have to turn the skills you didn't know you had into cash.

Writing and/or publishing a book is one of the few things that just about any-one can do – if they are prepared to put in the requisite amount of hard work.

Publishing and selling his own book gives the author a chance to take control of his own destiny. Any author who has confidence in the value of his own work ought to publish his or her own books. And anyone who can't write should become a publisher. It's the fastest, simplest route to independence and wealth.

The bottom line is simple: publishing can enable you to gain personal and financial independence.

Good luck!

Vernon Coleman

PS I ask you just one favour: in five years' time send me a postcard from your holiday home in the Caribbean. It will give me a kick to know how well you've succeeded.
PPS Some people in the publishing industry claim that authors only 'self-publish' because they can't get their books accepted by other publishers. This is nonsense. I've sold millions of books through 'ordinary' publishers – and I still use 'ordinary' publishing companies outside the UK and for mass market paperbacks (where distribution is crucial and difficult to match as a self publisher). I choose to self publish because it gives me more control and it's more fun. I make more money too.

HOW TO BE A PUBLISHER – PART ONE

'I suffer from the disease of writing books.' Charles Louis de Secondat, Baron de Montesquieu

WRITING YOUR BOOK (OR GETTING SOMEONE TO WRITE IT FOR YOU)

Contents

1. THE STARTING POINT: GETTING AN IDEA, AND CHOOSING THE SUBJECT FOR YOUR FIRST BOOK

Before you can write a book you need an idea. The quality of your book, whether it is to be a volume of fiction or non fiction, will to a very large extent depend upon the quality of your idea.

You may think that I am stating the obvious. Sadly, I am not. Not all books are born of passion. Some result from a commercial coupling between publisher and author, inspired by the computerised equivalent of the tinkle of cash registers.

The only two fundamental functions of any business (whether it be a professional offering knowledge or a skill, a service provider such as a hairdresser or an estate agent, a corner shop, a local business, a multinational business or an author selling his own books) are to create new products and to then sell those new products.

But people do not buy products or services: they buy ideas, hopes, solutions, time, concepts and dreams. The woman who goes into a hairdresser's salon isn't going there to get her hair cut. She is going there because she wants to look good. When people buy cars they are buying an 'image' as much as a means of transport. And the person who buys a book isn't buying a book; he or she is buying information, education, entertainment or a gift.

Your first step on the road towards making money through publishing should be to analyse and make an inventory of your intellectual assets. What are your special and most significant skills? Do you have special knowledge you can sell? Do you have knowledge or skills which you can define, promote and sell?

The first big problem with books (and the first reason why they are unique creations which present unique marketing problems) is that they are all different and their differences are created and defined by the idiosyncrasies, tastes, skills, frailties, egos and prejudices of their authors (and sometimes, when editorial work is unacceptably intrusive, by their editors too).

The second big problem with books (and the second reason why they are unique creations which present unique marketing problems) is that the people who read them are all different too – and all have their own very special needs, hopes, expectations, prejudices and egos. No two readers respond to a book (or an author) in exactly the same way. When someone reads a book they inevitably develop some sort of relationship with the author. And the way people interact when they meet one another varies constantly. Jack may like Jill but Dora may think Jill stinks. Dick may love Dora and Dora may love Dick but Jack and Jill may think that Dick is unbearable.

There is nothing quite so personal as the choice of a book to read (choosing a book as a gift is a very different exercise). People will happily buy chairs, beds, cars, lampshades and other items from a limited repertoire of opportunities. But when choosing a book they expect to be able to select from several thousand possibilities.

It is, therefore, quite impossible to say with certainty, that because there is a need for a book on train-spotting in Bavaria, commissioning a book on train-spotting in Bavaria will result in a steady and predictable sale. It may be true that there is a market for such a book but the book which is produced may not prove to be the book that people want to buy.

Marketing people claim that they can get around this problem by talking to people and finding out what they are reading. This is nonsense. People in different areas read different books. Their future buying habits are not necessarily influenced by what they have read in the past. And people lie about what they read in exactly the same way that they lie about how many cigarettes they smoke or how much alcohol they drink. (Ask most people what they have read recently and they will always give you the names of titles which they think will impress you – rather than the titles of the easy-to-read novels they have really been enjoying. How many people being interviewed for a job or university place will admit to reading and enjoying Jeffrey Archer?)

The marketing people claim that they can influence purchasing habits by demanding the right type of cover or the most alluring title. But not even doing this will guarantee a best-seller. The moment the marketing scientists think they know what colour covers are most attractive someone will break the mould and prove that public tastes have changed.

It has become fashionable in publishing to commission market research to find out whether or not there is a market for a proposed book. This is not a very bright thing to do. Commissioning effective market research may cost between £5,000 and £10,000. But it costs less than this to publish and print 1,000 copies of a book. And what better way is there to find out whether or not there is a market for a book than to print it and see if anyone wants to buy it? No amount of market research can really tell you whether or not there is a market for a book that hasn't yet been published. The main problem is that market research is based on the past. The people who are interviewed are questioned about what they might do – based on their past experiences. A new book is – or should be – a new experience.

The truth is that the only way to find out for sure whether or not there is a market for a book is to publish the book and try to sell it.

All this might sound rather depressing – as though publishing must inevitably be a hit and miss affair.

But this isn't entirely true.

Nothing – cover design, price, size, paper choice, editing – is anywhere near as important as what is in the book itself. A well-written book, written more out of a sense of passion than a desire to satisfy a market need, will always have a decent chance of finding a market. I would go further: a badly-edited, poorly-produced, overpriced book that is well-written with passion will, in the long-term, always sell better than a well-edited, well-produced, cheap book that is poorly-written and which has been composed without passion. Most important of all, a well-written book which has been written by an author prepared to put his or her passion on the page is the only sort of book that will acquire that one quality which establishes a book as a success: word of mouth recommendation.

Since I started publishing my own books I have followed one simple rule (actually, it is the same rule that I followed when I wrote books for other people to publish): I only write books that I want to write and that I can feel passionate about. I then put a little bit of my soul into the book. An author should bleed onto the page when he is writing for it is only through his blood that the book can come to life.

Only then, when I have written a book, do I worry about the format I will choose (should it be a hardback, a paperback, a booklet, an audio tape or a mixture of all those things) and about how I am going to find people to read it.

Personally, I write books that I want to write and then worry about how to sell them. This commercially suicidal approach seems to work for me. But if you want to begin by writing a book for which there is a proven market then you should know that diet books and books on how to make money are said to do particularly well. Books on animals tend to do well. Food, sex and health are also topics which generally go down well with readers.

If you are an expert on anything then that is undoubtedly the area to settle on for your first book. The subject doesn't matter – there is almost certain to be a market for a book on it if you can write knowledgeably and enthusiastically. Dog breeding, jam making, bird spotting, brass rubbing, book collecting, line dancing, collecting classic Bentleys, organic gardening – the list of possibilities is endless. If you can't think of anything to write about visit your local bookshop or local library, take a look at the books on the shelves and see if you can spot something that you would enjoy writing about.

If you want to write and sell fiction then that's perfectly possible too. Since I started writing and publishing my own fiction (I had four novels published by 'ortho-dox' publishers) I've sold over 100,000 copies of my own novels in hardback in the UK. That's far more than most novelists who are published by so-called 'orthodox' publishers.

There is only one type of book I can think of where you might have difficulty finding buyers: a serious, self-promoting autobiography.

An earnest book about your thirty years as a plumber, taxi driver, surgeon or hospital administrator is unlikely to be a best-seller unless you have a good many friends and relatives or you have a great sense of humour and a good turn of phrase. Autobiographies only work well if you've had a truly extraordinary life or experience, or can write a very funny book.

Remember that no one is going to buy (let alone read) your book unless there is something in it for them. Why should they? Would you read a book simply to delight the author?

People read books to be informed or entertained.

2. *Should you write your book yourself – or find someone to write it for you?*

Writing your own book has obvious advantages. First, of course, you don't have to pay a writer. You get to keep all the money. But that isn't really the main advantage. The big advantage is that you keep more control. You don't have to worry about a writer who gets distracted and misses his (and your) deadline. And, most important of all, you get a voice.

Most of us have effectively been disenfranchised. The politicians control our lives in a very intrusive way. Large international corporations push us all around as though we were so many grains of sand. And although they may claim to listen, most of the major media outlets (TV and radio stations, newspapers and magazines) exist to promote the interests of their corporate owners and their political friends.

Writing your own book will give you a voice – and a small amount of power in a world where most people are powerless. Maybe your book will be the one which triggers a revolution.

But not everyone finds writing easy. And not everyone wants to write their own book.

If you want to become a publisher but, for whatever reason, you don't want to become a writer, do not despair.

You can find yourself as many writers as you need without very much difficulty. The world is full of unpublished writers desperate to find a publisher.

3. How to write a best-seller

The first thing you must remember when you start writing a non fiction book is that most people buy non fiction books for one of two very simple reasons only: they either want to be entertained or they want information and advice. Try to decide which sort of book you want to write before you write it. This will help you write a better book.

If you decide to write a book based on your thirty years' experience as a school-teacher you will find the book easier to write if, before you start to hammer the keyboard, you know whether you intend to entertain your readers with rib-tickling anecdotes from your days in the classroom (*Thirty Years Of Chalk And Duster*) or you intend to provide neophyte school-teachers with a clear guide to the pitfalls which await them in a teaching career. (*How To Be A Successful And Happy Teacher*).

I am not, of course, suggesting that these two approaches are mutually exclusive. If you are writing a practical, informative guide book you should (if you can) try to make your book as readable and as entertaining as possible. There is no reason at all why a book bought for information shouldn't be fun to read. And the corollary is true too. If you are writing an autobiography there is no reason why your book should not be full of titbits of useful information.

But unless you have some idea of the sort of book you plan to write when you sit down and start writing the chances are that it will lack any sort of framework and, more important, a clear purpose.

I have in the past been shown numerous typescripts put together by would-be authors. The commonest problem I found was that although many of them were the right length to be books, they simply weren't books. There was nothing holding all the words together. There may have been twenty chapters, sixty thousand words and a foreword in the package. But twenty chapters, sixty thousand words and a foreword do not automatically make a book.

When writing a non fiction book you have to start with a purpose. Why do you want to write the book? Why do you have to write the book? Why is the book necessary?

When you know the answers to these simple questions you will find it relatively easy to work out what to put in the book.

4. Finding, hiring and dealing with an outside author

Since I first started publishing my own books my office has regularly received manuscripts, typescripts, disks and letters from authors wanting me to publish their books. People send me novels, autobiographies and books of non fiction. Some of the authors who want me to publish their book are first timers. Others are seasoned professionals who have published a number of books with so-called 'commercial' publishers.

All these manuscripts are returned to their authors with a letter wishing them the best of luck and explaining that I do not publish other people's books.

I decided some time ago that I was busy enough publishing my own books. Although I have become a publisher I still very much consider myself an author not a publisher.

But if I wanted to publish other people's books I would have absolutely no difficulty in finding plenty of suitable material.

Some of the manuscripts we are sent need a great deal of work. But others are excellent and could be published at a profit with hardly any work being done on them.

As soon as word gets around that you are a publisher you too will find yourself inundated with manuscripts and ideas for books.

Until that point comes you can find writers quite easily by putting small advertisements into the classified pages of appropriate publications.

If you decide that there is a market for a book on cricket and you want someone to write a book on cricket then put a small advertisement in the classified pages of a cricket magazine. If you want a book on local history put an advertisement in your local newspaper. And then stand back! You will probably receive far more applications than you can cope with. You will quickly find that the world is full of unpublished and would-be writers. There are nowhere near enough publishers to go around.

How do you pay your writer? That's your choice. You can either hand over a flat fee (a few hundred pounds will probably suffice) or a royalty based on the number of books sold. As the publisher you have control of everything – including the author and the money.

5. Do you need an editor?

Some critics of small publishers claim that the biggest problem is that small publishers have to manage without a good editor.

I fear that such critics are rather out of touch since good editing hasn't been regarded as an essential part of mainstream publishing for many years.

It is, of course, perfectly true that a good editor can greatly improve the balance and accessibility of anything that has been written. (And, at Publishing House, I have the best editors around.) But it is also true that no one ever buys a book, a newspaper or a magazine because it has been well edited.

Readers may (quite reasonably) moan if the publication is littered with misprints and painful grammatical errors but the simple fact is that editors are secondary to the whole business of writing. They are far, far less important than writers and much less important than printers. They are, in many ways, the most expendable part of the whole publishing business.

Sadly, many editors do not recognise their role in the whole hierarchical publishing system and rather give the impression that they consider themselves to be by far the most important figures in the business.

You and I know better.

A writer can write without an editor but an editor can't do anything without a writer.

When I used to publish the first editions of my books through London publishing houses I had numerous rows with extremely young and inexperienced (but uncritically, politically correct) graduates who thought that because they had a degree, had been on a weekend publishing course and had a plastic plaque with 'EDITOR' stamped on it on their door or desk, they automatically knew everything there was to know about books and publishing.

I lost count of the number of rows I had with snooty, half-baked decerebrates who thought that their few months' experience of being patronising to other authors gave them the right to tell me what to put into my book (and what to take out).

My favourite trick with these literary incompetents (most of the ones I met seemed, sadly, to have relatively little knowledge of how to use semi colons and commas but a good many politically correct views, though it was the first of these I was looking for) was to invite them to look at the title page of the book we were discussing.

'Whose name do you see there?' I would ask, as sweetly as I could manage.

'Yours,' the editor would reply, after a moment's hesitation.

'Exactly!' I would say. 'This is my book we are talking about. If you want to write your own book then please feel free to do so. I promise that I will not make any attempts to tell you what you can or cannot include in it.'

You will, of course, want to make sure that your book is as free of misprints and grammatical errors as you can make it. Don't bother with grammar check programmes offered by your computer or by software manufacturers. I haven't found one worth using. The spell check facility on most computers is, however, worth using.

Ask friends and relatives to read your typescript before you turn it into a book. And ask them to look out for errors. If you want to you can hire a professional proof reader. But in my experience friends and relatives will do just as well – if not better.

HOW TO BE A PUBLISHER – PART TWO

'As repressed sadists are supposed to become policemen or butchers so those with irrational fear of life become publishers.' CYRIL CONNOLLY

TURNING AN IDEA INTO A BOOK: THE PRACTICAL ASPECTS OF BOOK PRODUCTION

Contents

1. HOW MUCH IS ALL THIS GOING TO COST?

If you think that getting your book printed will be your only expense then you are dangerously wrong – and heading for disaster.

But once you have the printing costs for your book then you can start working out the costs for the other essentials.

Making a book involves seven basic costs:

a) The cost of printing and binding will usually be between a tenth and a fifth of the cover price. As a publisher there is nothing you can do about this expense. If your book costs you £1 to £2 to print and bind then you should probably charge £9.95 when you sell it. The printing and binding price is the foundation upon which you can work out the other costs involved in publishing a book. It is the cost of printing which means that publishing does require a modest initial capital outlay – although, since printers commonly give 60 days' credit to their customers it is, if you have strong nerves, perfectly possible to get your book printed and then rely on selling enough copies to pay the printer. If I was starting out I wouldn't like to do this. I would prefer to have the cash to pay my debts as I go, knowing that the profits, when they come, will be all mine. I'd do it this way even if it meant waiting for a while to build up the necessary capital.

Printing 1,000 copies of a proper paperback book will probably cost you between £2,000 and £3,000 but these costs are falling all the time. New technology means that there are now many printers around who will print just 100 copies of your book. You can even find printers who will print copies of your book as you need them. You don't order the books to be made until you've actually sold them!

b) You should allow another 10% of the cover price for distribution – whether you send your books out by the lorry load to bookshops and wholesalers or whether you post off books individually in padded bags. Once again this cost will be unavoidable. You have to distribute your books if you are going to sell them.

c) If you sell your book through wholesalers and retailers then you will have to give them between 35% and 50% of the published price. The small publisher can cut this cost by giving a lower percentage to bookshops – which will usually order single copies as customers order the book from them. Bookshops are unlikely to order from you in huge quantities. You can cut out wholesalers and give 15% to 20% to book-shops. If cash is paid up front then the money lost through bookshops refusing to pay their bills (or going bust) will be slight.

d) A normal publisher will allow around 10% of the published cost of a book for overheads (rent of premises, rates, salaries of staff, electricity, heating, telephone and so on). Compared to a publisher with posh offices in central London you will probably have relatively low costs in this area but you will have costs and these should be recorded among your expenses when you submit a tax return.

e) It is fairly normal to allow 7.5% of the published price for marketing and advertising. You should not skimp on this area of expenditure. You will probably not have a sales force and you will not need to buy huge self congratulatory advertise-ments in the trade press, but since mail order sales will play a vital part in your grow-ing business you must allocate money to buying advertisements in magazines and newspapers. The money saved on bookshop commission and overheads should be allocated to the advertising budget.

f) The author of a book will normally receive an average royalty of around 10% of the published price and most publishers pay their authors an advance against the estimated royalties that the book is expected to earn. The advance is usually bro-ken into three parts. One third is paid when the contract is signed, one third is paid when the book is delivered and the final third is handed over when the book is finally published. Publishers usually decide on the size of the advance after working out how many books they think they will sell – and what the author's accumulated royalties will amount to. So, assume that a book is to be published at £10 and the royalty level is 10%. This means that the author will receive £1 for every book sold. If the pub-lisher estimates that he will sell 3,000 books he will probably suggest an advance of £3,000 – to be divided into three parts, £1,000 to be paid when the contract is signed, £1,000 to be paid when the manuscript is received and the final £1,000 to be paid when the book is published. Publishers often wildly overestimate the amount a book will earn when handing out advances. It was reported recently that one large Ameri-can publisher wrote off about $80,000,000 worth of unearned advances while an-other wrote off close to $35,000,000 worth of unearned advances.

If you are writing your book yourself then you don't need to worry about hav-ing to pay an author a huge advance. You don't even have to worry about having to pay any royalties. If you hire an author to write your book(s) for you then you can either pay them a flat fee for the rights in the book you want to publish (a simpler arrangement than having to work out royalties, though this is not something I ever recommend to authors) or you can pay a traditional advance against royalties and then pay out royalties if and when the advance is exceeded.

g) A traditional publisher's final cost (and by far the most difficult to estimate) is the cost of returns. If a publisher ships vast quantities of a book in response to massive bookshop orders he may become too enthusiastic and reprint yet more books in the hope and expectation that the book is going to be a major best-seller. But if the bookshops return a high proportion of the books then the publisher is likely to be in deep, deep trouble. According to a recent issue of *New Yorker* magazine the average independent bookstore returns about 20% of its books whereas chains may have returns of 30% upwards. Around a third of all published adult trade hardback books are returned unsold in the US. Most of these books cannot be resold and unless they can find a home on the remainder tables they are simply destroyed. Astonishingly high returns (in excess of 50%) are by no means unknown and in the world of paperback publishing are fairly commonplace. The small publisher is unlikely to have high enough bookshop sales to have to worry much about returns.

If you find the financial implications of publishing rather frightening then I suggest that you consider the following simple facts which may help soothe your worries a little.

The first important thing you should remember is that all investment is gambling. If you have savings which you give to your bank to invest on your behalf then you are, whether you like the idea or not, gambling. You are gambling that the bank will not go bust. And you are gambling that your investment will gain value – rather than lose value. In some circumstances the risk may be slight. But it is foolish to pretend that there is no risk. And when you invest in someone else's business (as you do when you buy shares in a public company) you are handing over all management responsibility to a group of people you don't know and will probably never meet. If you invest in a unit trust or an investment trust then you are spreading your risk by putting your money into numerous companies but there is still an element of risk involved. On this occasion you are trusting the investment managers who decide which companies should benefit from your savings. If the investment manager is blessed with a brain the size of a dried pea your investment is likely to shrink rather than grow. (It is worth remembering that most people who entrust their savings to investment managers seem to do rather worse than individuals who simply invest their savings in a dozen or so blue chip shares. There is even some evidence to suggest that picking shares by throwing darts at the share price list in a newspaper will produce results just as good as those produced by expensive investment managers). If you decide that all this is too risky for you and you put your money in a sock and hide it under the bed then you are gambling that inflation will not eat into your savings. You will almost certainly lose this gamble and when you take the sock out your savings will have a much smaller buying value than they had when you put the sock under the bed.

You should remember all this when trying to decide whether or not to risk investing a little money in setting up your own publishing business.

When you publish a book you are backing your own skills. You are in a strong position to decide whether or not your publishing venture is a success. There are, of course, numerous outside factors over which you may have little or no control but which may determine the financial success of your venture. But, generally speaking, if you decide to publish your own book you will have far more control over the outcome than you will if you give your money to someone else to manage for you.

The second vital factor to remember is (as I have already pointed out) that when you publish your own book you can usually delay the moment when you have to find real money until after you have received the printed books and have begun to sell them. Since it is usually also possible to purchase advertisements on credit you may be able to publish your own book without any capital at all.

Having said this I must repeat that personally, I wouldn't like to do this and I would strongly recommend that you have all the money you are prepared to venture sitting in an interest-earning deposit account at the bank before you start publishing. However, the 60 days that you are likely to be able to wait before you pay the printer, and the 30 days that you may be able to wait before you pay the proprietor of the newspaper or magazine in which your advertisement appears, does give you a little extra room for manoeuvre.

The one time when you may find the credit periods of real value is when you publish your second book and find your publishing empire beginning to blossom. If your first book is just beginning to become profitable, and you have established advertisements which work and, maybe sold foreign rights or serial rights which will bring you in money in the future, then you may be grateful for the help with your cash flow. The help will enable you to increase your advertising budget and, maybe, order a reprint of your first book.

The third factor which you should remember (and which may help to influence your decision about whether or not to go it alone and publish your own book) is that if you publish your book with the genuine intention to make money out of the venture, then you will hopefully be allowed to offset the costs of your venture against any other freelance or self employed income you have when you have to declare your earnings to the tax man. Printing costs, postage, advertising costs, stationery costs and so on will all be deductible. If you have to go to Italy for two months to do research for a book then the costs will be deductible. You will, of course, have to keep a full record of your outgoings and your earnings but it is always nice to know that the Chancellor of the Exchequer (who will eventually share in your good fortune if your book makes a profit) will share with you the risk that your venture may make a loss.

Fourth, it is worth remembering that the government wants you to spend your money on frippery so that you remain a wage slave. Governments like people who spend all their money on things they don't really need for it is people who spend who help to keep the economy strong and if people only spent their money on essentials most folk wouldn't need to work more than a few hours a week. If your income and outgoings are balanced rather tightly and you feel nervous about publishing your own book then perhaps it might be worth taking a look at your outgoings to see whether or not you can cut anything from your weekly and monthly budgets. Publishing your own book might enable you to gain personal and financial independence for the first time in your life. You may feel such a goal makes a few short term sacrifices worthwhile.

2. KEEP EXPENSES DOWN – WHY YOU DON'T NEED AN EXPENSIVE OFFICE (AND WHY YOU DON'T EVEN NEED TO FORM A COMPANY)

Publishing books requires space. You can't do it from the kitchen table. (Well, I suppose you could. But unless you eat all your meals in restaurants and cafes I don't suggest that you try and run your new publishing empire from the kitchen table or the dining room table. If you do you will soon get fed up of getting everything out and putting it away and getting it out and putting it away. You will be spending more time getting ready to work than you will be spending on work and unless you live alone you will soon find your domestic arrangements under a certain amount of strain.)

Until your books arrive from the printers you will only need space for a computer, typewriter or writing pad and pen. But once the books arrive (and this is the point at which you will really feel that you are a publisher) you will need a lot of space. You will need somewhere to store the books. You will need somewhere to store the packaging in which you send out the books. You will need somewhere to process the orders and you will need somewhere to weigh parcels and stick on stamps.

Don't whatever you do rush round to your nearest estate agent and buy or rent an office. To begin with you can run everything from a spare bedroom. You don't need much more equipment to be a publisher than you need to write a letter. You need a desk, a typewriter or a computer, a telephone, a fax machine and an almost endless supply of paper and pens. I suggest you do have the luxury of two telephone lines – one for your telephone and one for the fax machine.

I believe fax machines are seriously under-estimated. If I had to choose between a telephone and a fax machine I'd choose the fax machine every time. You can send messages and proofs at any time of the day or night without having to worry about answering machines. Having one line for both fax and telephone always seems to me to be rather 'cheap' and 'amateurish' and is often a great nuisance both for you and for other people. You will, I think, find that two lines will both be more efficient and also more professional.

If you rush out and buy or rent a special office you will immediately burden yourself with the businessman's curse: significant overheads.

We had published half a dozen books (including the best sellers *Alice's Diary* and *The Village Cricket Tour*) before we invested in proper offices. Until that date everything had been run from home with between 15,000 and 20,000 hardback books stored in a barn and a garage. At busy times we would recruit everyone passing through to help open the mail and stick books in bags. Floors were left un-hoovered while the woman hired to look after the house stuck stamps on envelopes and parcelled up books.

Eventually it all became too much to run from home and we set about looking for a building which we could turn into a centre for a small but rapidly-blossoming empire. We were lucky to find a large shell of a building which we were able to turn into offices and a warehouse. It didn't take long to decide to call it Publishing House.

But even though my publishing imprints had acquired a proper home of their own I still didn't form a company.

My view is that becoming a company is probably quite unnecessary – unless you enjoy the extra administration and accounts associated with running a limited company.

I operate as a sole trader and there are, it seems to me, several advantages in working this way.

First, everything is kept relatively simple. At the end of each tax year I add up my income, take away the expenses and pay tax on what is left – the profit. I dispensed with my accountant some time ago and these days I fill in the forms myself. Doing your own accounts means that you have some idea of whether or not you are making a profit – and it means that you know exactly what you owe the tax man.

Second, if you run all your writing enterprises as one you may, when you are starting out, be able to set any losses you make through setting up your business against profits from your other self-employed activities. For example, if you earn money writing articles for newspapers and magazines or you provide money to pay for food by cleaning windows, you can set the costs of advertising your books against those earnings. If you set up a company to publish books your personal accounts and the company accounts will have to be kept apart and you will not have this flexibility.

The big advantage of operating a limited company is, of course, the fact that your own personal liabilities are limited. But in reality I'm not sure that this is much of a practical advantage. Being a limited company won't protect you if you publish something you've written which turns out to be libellous. The person you have libelled will simply sue you as the author rather than as the publisher. You can't escape from that responsibility. And since no one is likely to give your company credit unless you provide some sort of personal guarantee or security (your house, insurance policy or family jewels) you aren't likely to benefit all that much from having a limited company standing between you and your creditors. Besides, I wouldn't like the idea of using a limited company to help me avoid my personal debts.

3. GETTING YOUR BOOK PRINTED

I suggest that you do not try printing and binding your book yourself unless you are happy to confine yourself to publishing booklets, pamphlets and sweet little publications which look as though they have been put together by a couple of sixth-formers from the local school.

Every week I am sent copies of books which have been put together with the aid of desk top publishing packages and then printed and bound in booklet form (sometimes by the local printer but sometimes at home). I have a very strong suspicion that 99.99% of these publications are either given away to friends and relatives or stored in the garage or the loft until they go mouldy. A few may be sold at car boot sales or church bazaars but I doubt if many are sold to strangers. (You are a successful small publisher when you start selling your books to strangers.)

Booklets (held together with staples and without a proper spine) are fine if you are publishing purely for fun (or because you simply want to spread your word around a few friends) but if you are going to go to all the trouble of writing a book (as opposed to a booklet) then you should produce and print it properly.

Anything which contains more than 20,000 words really needs a proper spine – and that means a proper book printer. Persuading bookshops and libraries to take copies of a book that hasn't been published by a big name publisher is difficult enough. If you offer them something that looks like a home-cooked booklet you will be making life unbelievably difficult for yourself.

You will need an International Standard Book Numbering number (known as an ISBN) for your book so that the book can be identified by bookshops, librarians and so on. When you begin publishing write to The Standard Book Numbering Agency and they will send you a useful little booklet and a list of ISBN numbers for you to use. You may also decide that you need an ISBN bar code for the printer to put on the cover of your book. ISBN bar codes don't add a great deal to the design of a book cover but they are essential if you expect to sell a lot of books through bookshops.

Finding a sympathetic and understanding printer is vital. And it isn't too difficult. Many printing companies now have the sort of machinery which enables them to produce short runs of books. (It is probably fair to say that anything less than 1,000 copies of a book is a 'short run'.)

When you receive your finished books from the printers open half a dozen packs (books usually come wrapped – either in brown paper or, more usually these days, in transparent shrink wrap which is damned near impossible to tear open) and make sure that your book is printed properly. Look to see that the page numbers run sequentially, that the printer hasn't added one section of the book twice, that a chunk of the book isn't missing and that there is a decent amount of ink on all the appropriate pages and none at all on those pages where ink would be nothing but an embarrassment. If you do not do your quality control check now then you may discover a serious problem in a year's time.

4. Hardback or paperback?

Logically there is no sound reason for publishing hardback books. They cost more to print and therefore cost more to sell and yet the stuff that really matters (the words inside) is just the same as could be put into a paperback. But here, as in many other areas of publishing, there are factors other than logic to be taken into consideration.

The first reason for seriously considering hardback publication is that the publishing trade itself still doesn't regard paperbacks as 'proper' books. If you think I'm exaggerating about this then look at the book review page in just about any broadsheet newspaper. You will see that most of the coverage is reserved for hardback books. Paperback books (even original paperbacks which have never appeared in hardback and which might, therefore, expect to be treated in the same way as hardbacks) are reviewed, often rather patronisingly, in a little box tucked into a corner of the page. Similarly booksellers will usually reserve most, if not all, of the space in their shop windows for hardback books.

The second reason for publishing a book as a hardback is that you then have a chance of selling the paperback rights to a specialist (or even a mass market) paperback publisher. It is, of course, well known that paperback publishers will sometimes hand over cheques for vast amounts of money for the right to publish a particular book in paperback in their chosen territory.

Do not, however, get too excited by this possibility. Sadly, cruelly and unfairly it is unlikely that a paperback publisher will even deign to look at a book published by a small publisher (though it does happen – in some cases spectacularly).

The third, and by far the most important, reason for considering hardback publication is that a large percentage of books are bought as presents and a hardback book makes a better present than a paperback book. Well, that's not really true, of course. It doesn't make a better present at all because the most important bit of the book (the words) will be just as entertaining or as informative when packed inside a paperback cover as it will be when wrapped inside a hard cover and an expensive dust wrapper – it simply looks better in the hard cover. But perception is, if not everything, almost everything. When buying a present, many people decide how much they are going to spend before they decide what to buy. And a hardback book not only fits into more present buying budget categories but it also looks a lot more expensive than a paperback. It is this third reason which you should consider carefully.

Finally, if you publish a book as a hardback you can always publish a (cheaper) paperback edition later on.

My advice is simple: if you are publishing a book which you suspect may be bought and given as a present then you should seriously consider hardback publication. If, however, you are publishing a book which will be bought largely or exclusively for the information it contains then you should probably prefer paperback publication.

5. CHOOSING A TITLE

As a publisher you will, of course, appreciate that words are powerful and important. It is always vital to pick the right words. Do you think that Moses would have been as successful if he had come down from the mountain with Ten Suggestions or Nine Hints?

If your book is going to be successful then your title has to catch the eye and fire the potential reader's imagination. If you are selling a non fiction book then you should remember that you are selling solutions, not problems! (Most people have plenty of problems. It is solutions they want and need.) Your title will, to a large extent, be your shop window. It will appear in your catalogue and (hopefully) in other people's catalogues. It is all the browser will see when peering at a row of spines on books in his local bookshop. In a library (where books are often put onto shelves naked, without their dust wrappers, and invariably stacked so that only their spines are visible) the title is all the would-be reader sees. (It pays to do everything you possibly can to make sure that your books are borrowed frequently in libraries. You benefit financially through the Public Lending Right system. You also benefit because if your book is read a great deal it will eventually fall apart and have to be replaced. And if librarians see that one of your books is popular they will be more likely to stock another of your books. You will also benefit because when lots of people read your books some of them will talk about you, and spread the good word among their friends.)

So how do you choose a title?

To a large extent finding a good title is something of a knack. But it is a knack that can be acquired. The quickest and easiest way to discover which titles work best is to look around your own bookshelves (or the bookshelves in a local bookshop or library) and write down the titles which really grab you.

When you have done this write down all the benefits and advantages of your book on lots of separate pieces of paper. When you've finished look at all the words you have written down. You may see a title struggling to get out from everything you have written.

When trying to think of a title attempt to decide what your customers really want from you; what are their particular fears and hopes; how can you help them satisfy their dreams and conquer their fears?

Remember that your customers don't want to buy a book – they want to buy a solution to a problem. If the problem is the fact that they have a headache then they want you to help them get rid of their headache. If the problem is that they are overwhelmed with government forms then they want you to help them deal with the forms in less time. If they are bored then they want you to intrigue and entertain them.

There are no hard and fast rules when it comes to selecting a title.

Sometimes a very simple, prosaic and obvious title is best. There is little point in trying to be clever, and looking for a witty *double entendre*, if you are planning to write (or have written) a book which offers information or advice on a specific subject. My books about specific diseases usually have very simple titles (such as *How To Conquer Arthritis*, *Relief from Irritable Bowel Syndrome* and *High Blood Pressure*). My theory is that an individual who has arthritis, and who is looking for a book on the subject, knows exactly what he or she wants. A clever title might be missed as he or she scans the shelves.

There are over 7,000 books in print with the words 'How to...' in the title. Do not be afraid to use these two words if they are appropriate.

Sometimes a witty or clever title may be more appropriate. And sometimes you can produce a best-seller by thinking up an entirely new word. One of my most successful books is *Bodypower*. (I have always had to fight hard to persuade other publishers and catalogue writers to print the title as one word rather than as two words). After *Bodypower* had been a success I wrote *Mindpower* and *Spiritpower* – thereby giving me a trilogy.

6. SELECTING A COVER DESIGN

If you intend to sell most of your books by mail order then, in theory at least, cover design is not terribly important. By the time your readers see your book they will have already paid for it and unless your cover appears in your advertisements they will have done so without knowing what it looks like.

But, in my view, cover design does matter – however you intend to sell your books.

It matters for several important reasons.

First, although it is difficult to get bookshops to order and stock a book published by any small publisher it will be a great deal more difficult (and probably impossible) if the book cover is not attractive. You may find this hard to believe, and even harder to accept, but it is not at all unknown for large bookshops to decide whether or not to buy a book solely on the cover. The bookshop buyers who work this way claim that they simply don't have time to read all the books they are offered and that consequently they have to choose books according to how they look. They further excuse this seemingly barbaric policy by claiming that bookshop customers use a similar technique when deciding which book to buy.

I am afraid that to a certain extent they are right. Potential buyers certainly flick through a book, look at the contents list and (if there is one) the index and read the first paragraph and another sentence or two taken at random somewhere in the middle of the book, but it is the cover that gets more attention than anything else. And, surprisingly perhaps, it is the back cover that gets most attention. A staggering number of publishers still produce books that have entirely blank back covers. I consider this to be extraordinarily inept; it is akin to committing professional and commercial suicide. It is mostly hard cover publishers who produce books with nothing on the back but some paperback publishers produce covers which might just as well be blank.

Next, bookshops which want to sell as many books as possible always stock their books face on or face out so that the front cover of the book is fully visible. Look in any remainder shop or in a bookshop (such as those at a railway station, supermarket or petrol station) which relies on a fast turnover of books and you will see that they stock a high proportion of their titles face on. As I explained earlier experienced authors know how important it is that their books are displayed face on and it is for this reason that in large bookshops (particularly in certain parts of London) you will see authors furtively moving their books from bookshelves (where they are displayed with only the spine visible) to a display table (where the whole of the front cover can be seen). Not surprisingly, bookshops will not be enthusiastic about displaying a book face on if the cover is not attractive.

You may, at some time, want to use a photograph of your book cover in a catalogue. Or, if you are lucky enough to persuade a newspaper or magazine to review your book, they may want to reproduce the cover. If the cover is attractive then this will help to sell your book. If the cover is dull, boring and unattractive then a photograph of the cover could well be more of a hindrance than a help.

While on the topic of newspaper and magazine reviews it is worth mentioning that editors who are reviewing half a dozen books will often select just one cover to illustrate their feature. Literary editors as a breed may not be among the brightest people in the world but most are equipped with enough native cunning to realise that their page will look bright and attractive if they choose the most attractive and exciting cover available to them. If your book cover looks like the front of a telephone directory your book will be unlikely to receive this extra boost.

Next, even if you sell your books by mail order, if your book looks uninspiring, miserable and second rate the reader who takes your book out of the padded bag will be disappointed. And, being disappointed there is naturally a greater chance that he will not like your book. If he doesn't like your book he may send it back and ask for a refund. If this happens you will lose money because you will have paid to post the book to him and when the book comes back it will probably not be resaleable; he will obviously not recommend your book to anyone else (and since word of mouth recommendation is by far the best and most effective long term method of selling books you will therefore suffer commercially) and he is extremely unlikely to become a faithful long term customer.

You owe it to yourself (and your book) to give it a good cover. If you are proud of the way your book looks you will be much more enthusiastic about promoting it. If you feel rather ashamed of its seedy appearance you will not be able to do your book justice.

When designing your book cover (or, if it is a hardback, the dust jacket) do remember that the cover will eventually end up wrapped around the business part of the book. This will give you a much greater skill in cover design than is enjoyed by most people in publishing. Bizarrely most covers and jackets are conceived flat, designed flat and approved flat. No one ever seems to have the intelligence to take the proposed cover, wrap it around a book of roughly similar size to the book that is being planned and see what it looks like.

Don't have your book price printed on your book unless you are feeling very confident. Bookshops will want you to print your price on your cover because it makes life easier for them. But they are unlikely to do much to help you so why should you endanger your business to help them? If you print a price on a book cover and you want to increase the price then you will have to have a lot of stickers printed. And then you will have to find someone to stick them all on. And then someone will complain that you have increased the price of your book and you will probably get into trouble. There is bound to be a quango or a self-appointed voluntary body somewhere which does not approve of raising prices. (Such bodies are not infrequently manned and womanned largely by people who live on taxpayer's money and who never actually have to dirty their hands with anything so distasteful as having to earn a living.)

On the other hand, if you are feeling confident, putting a book price on a cover does have one big advantage: if you want to sell the book at a cheaper price your customers will be able to see exactly how much money they are saving.

It is possible that the people who print your covers will not be the same as the people who print your books. If this is the case you can save yourself a great deal of work and heartache by persuading the two companies to liaise and work together to make sure that everything goes smoothly. In particular, it is desperately important that the covers fit the books. The only thing sillier (and more annoying) than a dust jacket that either doesn't quite fit a hardback book, or else sticks out at the top or the bottom by a millimetre, is a paperback book cover that doesn't fit.

If you ask these two essential groups of people to work together you can avoid a great deal of responsibility. If something goes wrong and the jacket or cover doesn't fit the book you can quite reasonably blame the two sets of professionals and let them get on with apportioning blame, sorting out the excess costs and making sure that you receive books with the right covers as soon as possible.

When you order the covers for your book ask the printer to produce a few hundred more than you will need. You can use these for publicity and promotion. The run on cost of covers is extremely small and you will obtain a good promotional aid at a very low cost. If you are publishing a hardback book, with a dust jacket, ask the printer to produce yet more spare jackets. Keep these flat and safe somewhere and use them to replace covers which become ripped or marked. (Hardback books which are returned by bookshops or customers will usually have the dust jacket damaged. If you don't have a spare jacket to put on you won't be able to re-sell the book.)

7. HOW MANY SHOULD YOU PRINT?

Once you start getting quotes from printers you will be astonished to see just how cheap books can be when you order large quantities. If you order 500 copies of a book then each copy may cost you, say, £6. If you order 1,000 copies then each copy may cost you £4. Were you to order 5,000 copies then it is a fair bet that the unit price would crash to £1.25 each. And if you were to rashly order 10,000 copies then it is a fair bet that you would pay only around £1 each. A print order of 100,000 (if you ordered this many you would probably have to requisition every spare bedroom and garage in your neighbourhood for storage space) would bring your unit price down to a point where it could be measured in pence.

The reason for this is obvious. One of the biggest costs in printing a book is getting the book ready for the printing presses. Once the presses are rolling the cost of additional paper and the cost of allowing the presses to run for a short while longer is relatively small.

You should try hard to resist the temptation to attempt to bring down the unit cost of your book by printing more than you realistically think you will be able to sell.

Even if you are convinced that you have a sure-fire winner you should be cautious. Do not be embarrassed or ashamed to print just 1,000 copies of your first edition. Indeed, I would strongly suggest that your first print order should be no more than 1,000 copies of your book.

On two occasions I have allowed my enthusiasm to push me into printing more books than I should have. On both of these occasions the books were non fiction books published under the European Medical Journal imprint. On both occasions I was convinced that the contents and titles were so good that the books would be a huge success.

When I had finished writing *Power over Cancer* I was extremely excited. The book contained easily readable evidence showing readers exactly how they could avoid 80% of all cancers. It seemed to me that this was a book that everyone would want to read. And so I thought I was being pessimistic and cautious by limiting my initial print run to 3,000 books.

I then compounded that mistake by spending a relatively large amount of money promoting the book.

(Today, when I begin an advertising campaign I start with just one advertisement. If the advertisement works then I will put the same advertisement into another newspaper or magazine. But if the advertisement doesn't work (by that I mean it doesn't at least cover its costs) then I will abandon it and try something different.)

When *Power over Cancer* came from the printers I was desperate to get the book to as many people as possible. I believed that the book gave me a genuine chance to cut the incidence of cancer. I, and I think everyone else at Publishing House, felt excited by the book.

And so I arranged for advertisements to be put into several newspapers and magazines without any testing.

To make things even worse I sent off 28,000 copies of a direct mail 'selling letter' promoting *Power over Cancer* to readers on our mailing list. I simply didn't want to waste any time getting the information in *Power over Cancer* to as many people as possible.

(As with advertising space bought in newspapers and magazines, it is essential to test direct mail selling letters. We normally do test mailings of 4,000 names. Some, more cautious, mail order sales people prefer to test on 1,000 or even 600 names. Sending a leaflet to 28,531 people cost £9,985.85 so we clearly needed to sell around 1,000 books at £9.95 to cover the cost of the mailshot alone. Spending such a lot of money on an untested mailshot was poor judgement. Incidentally, at the time when we did that mailing the average cost of a mailing in the UK was 44 pence when the cost of the postage and the cost of the brochure, envelope etc. were added together.)

The attempts to sell the book were a disaster. We lost money on every advertisement we bought and we lost money on the mailshot. As far as the mailshot is concerned we were saved only by the fact that we had routinely included a copy of our catalogue with the selling letter for *Power over Cancer*. We received a good response to the catalogue and this paid for the cost of the stamps and the mailing.

Nothing saved the press advertisements from failure. An advertisement in *The Daily Telegraph* which cost £1,000 (plus the cost of preparing the advertisement) brought in a grand total of £318 worth of orders. Out of that £318 we had to pay for the books we sent out and the postage to send out the books. An advertisement in *The Guardian* cost £450 and brought in £109. An advertisement in *The Independent* cost £450 and brought in £189. And an advertisement in the magazine *Prima* cost £600 and brought in £199. Further tests proved to be just as disappointing.

If *Power over Cancer* had been my first venture into book publishing and I had not had the income from other, more successful books to help pay for this disaster my recklessness in not testing the book properly could have put an end to my publishing career.

We have slowly (over more than two years) got rid of all of the 3,000 copies of *Power over Cancer* that were printed but the book has not been a commercial success.

Our other notable failure was *How To Stop Your Doctor Killing You*. This time I was convinced that the title would be a winner. Everyone who saw the book cover seemed to think it was bound to be a success. (Maybe that should have warned me that all would not be well.) And overseas publishers jump at the book when they see the cover – choosing to buy it even when I tell them that other, less exciting sounding titles, sell much better.

I printed 3,000 copies of *How To Stop Your Doctor Killing You* but this time I was more cautious about buying advertisements.

My initial advertisement spend was just £1,700. This was made up of £1,200 for an advertisement in *The Daily Telegraph* (which brought in a total of £1,094) and

£500 for an advertisement in *The Guardian* (which brought in just £278).

When looking at these figures you must remember that an advertisement that costs £1,000 has to bring in about £1,500 worth of orders before it becomes profitable because to the cost of the advertisement itself you must always add the cost of the books you are sending out, the cost of the postage, the cost of the padded bag and the cost of paying someone to type the purchasers' details into the computer, the cost of buying labels, the cost of sticking labels onto padded bags, the cost of putting the books into the padded bags, the cost of putting the cheques into the bank and all the relevant overheads.

Why were these two books commercial failures?

I'm not sure, though I have some ideas.

I suspect that *Power over Cancer* did not sell well because most people don't want to know how to avoid cancer. They don't even want to think about cancer. They would rather wait until they get it and then rely on doctors to cure it for them with drugs, surgery and radiotherapy.

And I suspect that *How To Stop Your Doctor Killing You* flopped because most people don't like to think that their doctor is an incompetent buffoon who is likely to kill them (even though the facts show that this is the case). Most people may accept that other people's doctors are buffoons but they prefer to think of their doctor as a wise man whom they can trust and who will save their lives through his diagnostic and prescribing skills if they fall ill. As long as their doctor seems to know their name and smiles at them when they enter the consulting room they will trust him and do anything he tells them to do.

I have published one or two other books which have failed to make money. But I have usually known in advance that the books were unlikely to make money.

For example, when I published *Fighting for Animals*, which deals with animal rights, I was not surprised when I could not sell the books even when I discounted the price to £2.95 (at which point I was making a considerable loss on the books).

Because I had published *Fighting for Animals* out of passion rather than out of any commercial logic I only printed 1,000 copies. Most of these have been given away rather than sold and as long as they are read that is fine by me.

To summarise: my mistake with *Power over Cancer* and *How To Stop Your Doctor Killing You* was to print too many books. Over eagerness and over confidence increased the risk of financial loss – although I am pleased to say that in both cases we escaped without a loss (and, indeed, made decent profits) by selling serial rights and foreign rights.

8. HOW MUCH SHOULD YOU CHARGE FOR YOUR BOOK?

Conventional publishers tend to underprice their books because they don't really understand what they are selling. Through sheer ignorance they quite wrongly assume that the only way that they can compete with other publishers is by cutting their prices and charging as little as possible. Every publisher who charges too little for their books is perpetuating the problem and creating for themselves, and everyone else, a structure which will ensure that the variety of books they can offer will always be strictly limited.

As a small publisher you may not sell as many copies as you might if the book was published by an orthodox, traditional publisher. But you can nevertheless make more money. Most big publishers tend to sell their books far too cheaply.

So, for example, consider my non-existent friend Jack Middleton who has written a book called *Dine from your Garden* in which he explains how he and his family grow all the fruit and vegetables they need in a small suburban garden simply by planning carefully and rotating their crops.

If Jack's book is published by Bigthick Books they may (if they are extremely successful) sell 3,000 copies of a paperback edition which they will sell at £3.95. Of the £11,850 that the book brings in Jack will probably receive 7.5% or £888.75. If Jack has received an advance for his book the advance will have to be paid off before he receives any royalties.

In contrast the retail bookshops and wholesale outlets will receive about half the total sum received – or £6,000. The rest of the income produced by the book will be swallowed up in paying the publishing company's fixed costs and providing it with a small profit. On a book like this there will probably be virtually no money at all spent on publicity and advertising.

If, on the other hand, Jack decides to print 1,000 copies of his book and sell the books himself at £9.95 he will only need to make 10% profit on the sales in order to make more money than he would receive from Bigthick Books. If he sells some of his books direct (without going through bookshops) he will save the 50% that bookshops and wholesalers take. And by publishing himself he will save the money the publisher has to pay in salaries, expenses, rates, rent and so on.

Small publishers tend to sell their books in smaller quantities. But the profit potential is usually much higher.

The only way that publishers can keep book prices as low as they are at the moment is by printing huge quantities of each book. The basic, most fundamental cost in book production is, inevitably, the cost of printing and binding the book. When print orders go up unit cost goes down and in order to make a profit on a book that sells for £2.95 publishers have to print in huge numbers. This obviously restricts the number and type of books that a publisher is likely to publish.

The result is that no orthodox, modern commercial publishing house is going to publish a controversial, risky book because they can't fit it into their system. Even if the book is extremely important they won't print it if they don't think they will sell enough copies to make the book viable within their publishing structure. They can't print 100,000 copies and charge £2.95 because they are frightened that they will be left with 99,000 unsold copies. And they can't print 1,000 copies and charge £9.95 because the booksellers (and the people who normally buy their books) expect them to charge £2.95 for a book.

The price of printing and binding your book is not, of course, the only factor you must take into consideration when deciding what to charge. You have to include costs for preparing the text ready for printing, preparing and printing a cover, transporting and storing your books and, of course, marketing, promoting and selling your books.

It is this final item which many publishers forget. The printer tells them that printing 1,000 copies of their book will cost £1,750 to print. They work out that this is £1.75 per book and assume that they can safely make a profit (or, at least, cover their costs) if they charge £2.95.

When they discover that their local bookshop wants a 40% discount and that the bill for printing a few leaflets and buying one relatively small advertisement in an appropriate publication will cost them £1,000 they begin to panic. The panic turns to terror when they realise that if they sell their book through the post they will have to give lots of money to the Post Office (which is always reluctant to give away stamps for free). And then there will also be the cost of buying padded bags in which the book can be posted. And there will also be the cost of paying someone to put the books into the padded bags. And then there is the cost of hiring someone to stick the address labels and the stamps on the outside of the padded bags.

(I heard of one author who published 1,000 copies of his own book. The books cost £4 each to produce and he offered them for retail sale at £5.95. When a large book chain offered to buy 500 copies on sale or return but wanted a 50% discount he had to turn down the offer because he would have made a large loss on the deal. In my view either his print and production costs were too high or else his retail price was too low.)

The easiest way to save money is, of course, by not advertising and not sending out any leaflets or brochures promoting your book. Do this and you'll end up with unsold stacks of books piled high in the spare bedroom and the garage. (A stack of just 1,000 books takes up a great deal of space. If you doubt me then I suggest that you collect together 100 books and see how much space they take up. At Publishing House we usually have between 30,000 and 40,000 books in stock at any one time.)

***

Choosing a price may seem daunting but, as is the case with so many other areas of publishing, other people have already done all the hard work for you.

The first thing you should know is that you should always end your price with the figures 95.

If you want to charge approximately £10 for a book then you should charge ·£9.95.

Don't make the error (made by so many big publishers) of charging £9.99. You may think that you will make another 4 pence a book and that if you sell 1,000 books you will add £40 to your bottom line profits.

This is a big mistake.

Book buyers will think of £9.95 as £9 (and therefore less than £10). But they will 'see' £9.99 as £10. And your sales will be reduced.

Take advantage of the years of research done by some of the world's biggest mail order publishers. Mail order publishers know what readers want because they get immediate feedback as a result of their advertisements and because it is possible to measure very precisely the success or failure of every book and every advert.

After experimenting with book prices mail order publishers have come to the conclusion that a book price should be one of the following: £9.95, £12.95, £15.95. £19.95, £24.95, £29.95, £34.95 or (and unless you are selling a highly technical book which is likely to appeal to a very small, wealthy audience this is more of a price for a report or a set of tapes than a single book) £39.95.

Don't ask me why this is. I don't know and I don't think anyone else does either. And it doesn't matter. I could give you all sorts of pseudo-logical arguments about why £12.95 seems close to £10 but £13.95 seems closer to £20 but life is too short to get stuck on trivia and commercial psychobabble. Just say a quiet 'thank you' to the mail order publishers who have spent vast amounts of money experimenting in order to find the right prices.

You should not, in my opinion, consider a cover price of less than £9.95 for any book you publish. A rule of thumb that used to be popular among publishers many years ago was that you should charge five times the total production cost (including printing costs and overheads). Because of rises in other costs this is now completely out of date and many publishers prefer to charge up to nine or ten times the basic printing cost. If this turns out to be too high you can always reduce it later. More importantly, you can reduce the price when you sell your book to special groups of customers. I suggest that if you want to reduce the price of your book when selling it on 'special offer' you take it down to either £7.95 or £5.95.

If you start out by pricing your book at £5.95 you will have no room to manoeuvre if you want to sell the book at a cheaper price.

If you venture into direct selling (as all author publishers should eventually) by sending leaflets and catalogues out to potential book buyers you will soon realise that the price of your book has to be at least £9.95.

Buying a mailing list of names may cost you anything between £100 and £400 for a thousand names. (The cost varies according to the list you are buying. By and large the more specific and exclusive the list, the higher the price will be. If you are buying a list of names and addresses of people who have bought books on fishing within the last 6 months, who regularly visit Scotland and who have an annual income in excess of £100,000 then you must expect to pay a high rate. If, on the other hand you are simply buying a list of people who have bought something by mail order in the last three years you will pay far less.)

To this must be added the costs of writing, designing and printing a brochure, buying envelopes, having the brochures stuffed into the envelopes, having the labels stuck onto the envelopes and then having the stuffed, labelled and sealed envelopes posted to their destination.

All this will put the cost of your mailing up to an average of around 44 pence per letter. (It will be considerably higher if your brochure is large, colourful and expensive. It will be rather less if you cut your costs to the bone.)

A 3% response from a mailshot is considered quite good in the direct mail business. (For a cold mailshot – sent to people with whom you have never done business before and who have no record of having bought books by mail order – a 2% response would be considered more normal.)

So, let's look at some practical figures.

Assume that you send out 1,000 leaflets for your new book *How To Enjoy Skiing In East Anglia*. The mailshot costs you £440 for leaflets and postage and buying the names and addresses costs you another £200. Your total expenditure is, therefore £640.

If 3% of the people you have mailed buy your book and your book costs £9.95 your gross income will be 30 x £9.95 = £298.50. To this must be added the cost of the books you had printed and have sent out. Sadly, some of the people who buy your book will take advantage of your money back guarantee and demand their money back.

This is what is known technically as a 'Whoops Oh Dear Response.' You will have found a great way to lose money.

There is probably no way for you to cut your basic costs (you have to pay the

Post Office, you have to have a leaflet printed) but there are three clear ways to turn this loss making situation into a profitable opportunity.

The first thing you can do is to try and reduce your controllable costs.

Tell the people renting you the 1,000 names and addresses that you can't afford to pay £200 but that you will pay them £100 and, if your test works, you will come back to them to buy more names. There is a good chance that they will agree to this.

And, instead of having a colour leaflet, get your printer to produce something printed in coloured ink on tinted paper. This may help you cut 5 pence a leaflet off the cost of producing and sending out your leaflets.

Your costs will now be cut to £390 (for printing and sending out the leaflets) plus £100 for renting the names and addresses of potential customers. Your total costs have been cut from £640 to £490. You have already saved £150 and things are looking much brighter.

The second thing you can do is to try to increase the number of people who respond positively to your leaflet and decide to buy your book. You can't do this by reducing your price because if you bring your price down you will have to sell even more books. And so the only way you can do this is to write a better leaflet.

And the third way to try to make a profit out of direct selling is by increasing the price of your book. If you put the price of your book up to £19.95 and you still get a 3% response your gross earnings will be £598.50. The problem here, of course, is that in order to make your book look worth £19.95 you will probably have to increase your production costs fairly dramatically.

If you can do a little of both – get a higher response from the people you have mailed and put your price up a little – then your chances of success become higher.

So, for example, you might decide to increase the price of your book to £12.95 (at which level you can probably get away without any major change in your production costs) while at the same time improving your leaflet so that you get a 6% response from the people you have mailed.

Now look at the figures.

A 6% response will mean that 60 of your 1,000 potential customers each send you a cheque for £12.95. That will give you a total income of £777.

If you assume that each book has cost you £3 to print and that you have to pay another £1 postage and packing to send out each book then the cost of sending out 60 books will be £240.

Your total costs are, therefore, £490 (for the mailing) and £240 (for the books you sold). This adds up to £730. And since your gross income was £777 you have made a profit.

Congratulations. (But don't forget that if, say, two people don't like your book and ask for their money back your income will be reduced to around £750 – giving you a profit of £20.)

Now, a profit of £20 doesn't sound much for all that work.

But this was, after all, a test.

Your next move is to use the money you have received from this test to help you rent 4,000 names and do a slightly bigger mailing.

If that bigger mailing works you then continue to do more and more mailings.

If you can eventually mail 50,000 names with the same leaflet you could end up with a profit of 50 x £20 which is £600 and, I'm sure you will agree, a little more worthwhile.

But just imagine how difficult it would have been to make ends meet (let alone make money) if you had decided to sell your book for £3.95!

Finally, here's something worth remembering: if you have 1,000 books printed and your print bill is £2,500 then each book costs £2.50 to print. But the books will really have only cost £2.50 if you sell them all. If you only sell 500 books (and give away the rest) then each book will have cost you £5. Remember this when working out costs.

When you have published your book you will suddenly find that lots and lots of people who have never written a book nor published one will suddenly seem to know a great deal more than you do about what the publication price should be. In particular you should be prepared for the fact that journalists who write reviews of your book will probably make snide remarks about the price. 'Great book but what a pity about the price,' they will write. You will want to write back and explain the costs involved in book production. Don't bother.

As a postscript to this section I have to tell you that putting too low a price on a book (or, indeed, any other product) can sometimes damage the sales. And putting a higher price on a book can increase the sales. At one point we tested the subscription price for *Dr Vernon Coleman's Health Letter*. We mailed one group of book buyers offering the newsletter at £35.95 and another group of book buyers offering them the newsletter at £39.95. Much to our astonishment the £39.95 mailshot proved by far the most effective – bringing in far more new subscribers than the mailshot offering the newsletter at £35.95. The difference was so great that it was quite clear that the higher price made the newsletter more attractive.

9. DON'T FORGET TO REGISTER YOUR COPYRIGHT

In order to register your copyright you must ensure that you put the appropriate lines at the beginning of each edition of your books.

I use the following words:

'The right of Vernon Coleman to be identified as the author of this work has been asserted in accordance with the Copyright, Designs and Parents Act 1988.'

'All rights reserved. No part of this book may be reproduced, stored in a retrieval system or transmitted, in any form or by any means electronic, mechanical, photocopying, recording or otherwise without the prior permission in writing of the publisher. This book is sold subject to the condition that it shall not by way of trade or otherwise be lent, re-sold, hired out or otherwise circulated without the publisher's prior consent in any form of binding or cover other than that in which it is published.'

If you look among the prelims in other books you will see that other publishers use a number of variations on these simple themes. The words have a vaguely impenetrable air about them which suggests that they may have some standing in law. I think that perhaps we should add a few hereuntos and wherefores to our clauses. These can, I believe, be purchased second hand at very reasonable prices from solicitors everywhere.

In addition to this note at the front of every book I have also taken the precaution of patenting my name and the name of my main publishing imprint.

Finally, as part of the copyright establishing process, every time you publish a new book you must send free copies to various major libraries.

HOW TO BE A PUBLISHER – PART THREE

'A living is made, Mr Kemper, by selling something that everybody needs at least once a year. Yes, sir! And a million is made by producing something that everybody needs every day. You artists produce something that nobody needs at any time.'

THORNTON WILDER, 'THE MATCHMAKER II'

HOW TO SELL YOUR BOOKS

Contents

Introduction

INTRODUCTION

Getting your book printed is the easy part. As the publisher you will be paying out money and so you won't have much trouble finding a printer to make you some books.

Selling and distribution are the difficult bits of the exercise. As anyone who has ever bought and sold a house will know buying is much easier than selling. When you are buying everyone wants to be nice to you and to help you. When you are selling life suddenly becomes a good deal more difficult.

Most small publishers make one big mistake: they spend most of their money on printing their book and allocate very little towards selling it.

It may be rather nice to imagine that you can write a book, have it printed, stack the published volumes neatly in your spare bedroom and in the garage and then sit back and wait for buyers to beat a path to your door. Sadly, it won't happen. If you want to sell your books you have to put time, effort and (I'm afraid) money into advertising and promoting your book.

You should never spend more than half of your overall publishing budget on printing. In other words you should never publish a book without being prepared to spend the same amount of money on advertising and promotion as you spent on printing.

The alternative is to take the truly amateur route. Keep your books stacked up in the garage and the spare bedroom and hand them as Christmas and birthday presents to all your friends and relatives. If you didn't print too many copies and you also donate copies of your book to local good causes (e.g. the Church jumble sale) you should manage to get rid of a third of your stock in thirty or forty years.

My guess (and hope) is that you're not interested in that alternative. You want to be a proper publisher. You want to sell books and make money. You want to find out how you can set up a publishing business which will earn you money while you sit watching television. Read on!

1. SELLING TO BOOKSHOPS

I will deal with bookshops first because most people who don't know very much about books and publishing probably imagine that if you are going to sell books you need to sell them through bookshops.

This is a myth.

You aren't going to sell many books through bookshops. And bookshops are steadily becoming less and less important in the world of publishing.

There are around 3,000 privately owned bookshops in the UK (plus all the chain bookshops, plus all the corner shops that stock some books) but half of these have a minuscule turnover. Reaching the managers and buying departments in all these bookshops (and then persuading them to purchase your book for their shelves) is one of the most difficult parts of traditional publishing.

Large, orthodox publishers maintain teams of sales representatives who trail constantly around the country calling in at bookshops and trying to persuade them to take copies of the books on their latest list.

By contrast, all small publishing enterprises have a tremendous amount of difficulty in trying to persuade bookshops to take their books.

On the (probably relatively rare) occasions when you do sell your books to bookshops you will be expected to offer a very good discount (a quarter off the price on single copy orders and between a third and a half off the published price on larger orders – some wholesalers insist on even bigger discounts). You will also have to pay to have your books delivered to the bookshops. You will probably find that you will, over the months and years, acquire a number of bad debts from bookshops. Some large chains of bookshops are very slow to pay. And a surprisingly large number of bookshops go bust.

I confess I find it difficult to understand how any bookshop can ever go bankrupt because bookshops usually buy books from a publisher on a 'sale or return' basis. What this means is that if the bookshop can't sell a book they will send it back to the publisher and demand a refund. This means that bookshops take no risk and have absolutely nothing to lose. They can order your books without any risk whatsoever. If they buy a book and then decide (seventeen years later when the book is dusty and out of date) that they don't want it, they simply send the book back and demand a refund. They will either expect a refund in cash or in the form of other, different books which they can try to sell.

Naturally, most publishers prefer to sell a book on a 'firm' sale basis as often as possible since this means that the bookshop cannot return the book if he doesn't manage to sell it. It is often better to give a bookshop a larger discount for a firm 'no returns' payment than give a smaller discount and allow the bookshop to return the book if they don't sell it. Books which are returned by bookshops are often unsaleable since they may be battered and have torn covers.

The saddest thing about the 'returns' policy as practised by many bookshops today is that books are given such a short time to succeed. I wouldn't really mind if bookshops gave books seventeen years on their shelves before deciding that they weren't going to sell. But some bookshops now send books back after they have had them on display (unsold) for a week. Three months is probably more usual but even three months isn't very long – it certainly doesn't give a book much of a chance to sell by 'word of mouth'.

With this huge advantage you would, as I've suggested, think it would be impossible for a bookshop to go bust. But they do. So beware. And if you are at all doubtful insist that the bookshop sends you the cheque before you send them the book. Indeed, it is often wise to ask for payment in advance if you haven't done business with a bookshop before. Bad debts can be a serious problem for the small publisher. Since many (or even most) of your sales will have resulted from customers walking into the bookshop and ordering your book it is perfectly reasonable to get the money from the bookshop before you send out the book.

We spend a fortune on advertising (in one single recent year of publishing we bought around £500,000 worth of advertising space in newspapers and magazines and bought a considerable amount of space in trade journals advertising directly to bookshops) but despite this bookshops are extremely unwilling to take our books unless they have been ordered specifically by a customer.

You might imagine that small bookshops in particular would welcome small publishers. After all, small publishers are helping to weaken the stranglehold that large publishing houses have on bookshops. The bigger a publisher is the easier it is for it to take a firm 'take it or leave it' attitude with bookshops when negotiating discounts.

But, to my great sadness, it seems that the proprietors of many small bookshops find small publishers too much trouble to deal with.

One bookshop once telephoned on a Monday to order a copy of *Alice's Diary* for a customer. We accepted the order (on credit) and posted the book. On the following day they rang again and ordered another copy of the same book. We accepted their order and posted a second book. On the Wednesday they rang again. This time they had two orders for *Alice's Diary*. We posted them two books. When they rang on the Thursday to order another copy we asked if they would like to take a few copies on sale or return. We said that this would enable them to have a better discount, it would mean that they would be able to supply their customers immediately and, if they put the books on their shelves, it might mean that they would sell a few additional copies. Despite the fact that this involved them in absolutely no risk whatsoever (we would have taken all the risk by sending the books to them on sale or return – if they didn't sell the books they wouldn't have to pay us for them but could simply return them) they did not think that this was a good idea.

It is the attitude of bookshops (and small bookshops in particular) which explains why we (in common with a growing number of small publishers) sell many of our books by mail order.

Even more frustrating as far as we are concerned are those bookshops who insist that our books simply do not exist. We regularly get telephone calls from would-be purchasers who tell us that they have visited every bookshop for miles around and have been told that *Alice's Diary* (or whatever other title they are asking for) does not exist. All our books are listed on computers, microfiche and in every reference book we can find; we sell thousands of books and advertise widely, regularly and expensively. And still there are bookshops who insist that our books don't exist. You will have the same problem.

***

Bookshop owners and managers (and bookshop assistants) often like to give the impression that they are providing society with a very special service.

They sometimes seem to regard themselves as being an important part of the complex structure which helps authors communicate with their readers. This, of course, is absolute twaddle and would fit quite nicely into one of those delightful little works of fiction composed by the Grimm brothers or by Mr Hans Christian Anderson.

Nothing illustrates better the failure of many modern booksellers to understand the needs and wants of the reading public than their appallingly self-serving habit of organising books by publisher. I don't think that booksellers genuinely think that members of the public really want to choose a book just because it has been published by a particular publisher – but they do enjoy the extra money they get from renting out shelf space by the yard to publishers who want to be sure that their books are well displayed and all neatly gathered together. Generally speaking readers look for books by subject or by author. With a few notable exceptions (Mills and Boon is a good example because it has such a well defined brand image that readers have a pretty good idea what they're going to get) they don't give a damn who published the book.

The simple but frequently denied truth is that bookshops are no more than retail outlets – and most of them are hugely incompetent retail outlets. The only thing that separates bookshops, and those who work in them, from shops selling shoes or baked beans is that bookshops are so grossly inefficient, and are run with such appalling incompetence, that if they were in any other line of business they would have all gone under years ago. Only the absurd over generosity of publishing companies has helped keep bookshops alive at all.

Those who run bookshops claim that their business is uniquely difficult because they have to stock so many different lines. This simply shows that the people who run bookshops are so out of touch with real life that they don't even do their own grocery shopping. If they would tiptoe down from their ivory towers for long enough to venture into a local corner shop they would realise how hollow this argument really is. (The fatuousness of this traditional 'bookselling is different because we have to stock so many different lines' argument is enhanced by the fact that whereas books have an almost indefinite shelf life the sort of products sold by the average corner shop have a very limited shelf life. Fruits and vegetables go off very quickly and daily newspapers have to be replaced and renewed on – surprise, surprise – a daily basis.)

None of this need concern you too much for the very simple but important reason that I am afraid that the importance of bookshops in the selling of books is rapidly diminishing. Within a year or two bookshops will be little more than historical anomalies, visited almost exclusively by the curious, by history students, by those looking for somewhere to shelter from the rain and by those with time to spare. Bookshops will be used for browsing and reading more than for book buying.

Bookshops will not be put out of business by the internet (though some bookshop owners, mistakenly assuming that selling books on the internet is a major threat to their existence are already setting up their own subsidiaries on the internet) because the internet is at the moment an over-hyped piece of technological nonsense which is viewed only by a limited number of computer users, many of whom are illiterate nerds who wouldn't know how to open a book if you handed them one.

Bookshops (and, indeed, many orthodox, well established publishing companies) are being put out of business by mail order and direct mail book selling. Most of them are so stupid and out of touch that they don't know it is happening. And the few who know it is happening are doing nothing at all about it. You, on the other hand, will very soon know the future of publishing and bookselling.

2. Mail order sales

The book trade regards mail order and direct mail bookselling as so distasteful that it has, for years, more or less tried to pretend that it doesn't happen and that if it does happen it certainly isn't anything that a 'proper' publisher would want to be associated with. 'He sells his books by mail order' and 'He is a mail order publisher' are always used in a derogatory way.

To some people in the world of publishing and literary criticism it seems as if mail order sales somehow don't really count. It is as though selling books by mail order is cheating – like digging out the seam of a cricket ball or giving your golf ball a helpful kick if it has found an unplayable lie.

The large, colourful advertisements for book clubs are tolerated on the grounds that they only appear in the more reputable magazines. Besides, it is widely believed that they help to accustom non book buyers to the idea of books and some of the most naive (or perhaps 'stupid' would be a more appropriate word) authors, publishers and bookshops believe that readers are likely to be encouraged to pop into their local bookshop when they see a book club advertisement.

I don't believe that many readers will go into a bookshop to order a book which they can obtain at a vastly reduced price from a book club simply by filling in a coupon or picking up the telephone.

Those of us who sell books by mail order can take advantage of the fact that many of our customers undoubtedly find bookshops daunting. Only a relatively small proportion of the population ever visit bookshops at all but those who do know that it is often difficult to find what you want even when you get there, that there may be long queues at the check-out desk, that ordering books can be difficult if not impossible and that the staff may too often be intimidating and far too busy chatting to bother themselves with actually selling a book.

As if all these advantages were not enough, those selling books by mail order often go one considerable step further and offer their customers a money-back-if-not-satisfied guarantee.

It is perhaps hardly surprising that bookshops constantly demand bigger margins and better terms from small publishers (who cannot afford to give them but invariably give in because they don't know what else to do) and yet still manage to make a loss.

You don't have to worry too much about bookshop discounts. You're going to make your money by selling books via mail order. And this is how you're going to make money while watching TV. You put your advert in a national newspaper or magazine. You hire a telephone answering service to take the calls, and write down your customers' credit card details. You hire a fulfilment company to send out the books. And you sit down, turn on the TV and wait for the money to pour in.

3. Direct mail

In October 1997 *The Bookseller* (a magazine which is usually known as the organ of the book trade though the modern bookselling business is so feeble and emasculated that I can't believe it really needs an organ) published an article entitled *The Direct Approach* in which a journalist reported that: 'Direct selling has been something of a fringe activity in publishing for many years. The main practitioners are the small independents with high-value niche books, for example publishers of technical directories, specialist financial titles or those publishing for the top end of the hobbyists market.' In my view direct selling is an important part of the future of publishing.

The term mail order selling covers all the different ways of selling through the mail (though it is usually used to refer to selling 'off the page' through newspaper and magazine advertisements).

But direct mail selling is very specific. Instead of putting an advertisement in a magazine or newspaper (or on television or the radio or whatever other medium you can think of) the publisher sends a selling letter, together with a brochure of some kind describing one or more books, direct to people who he thinks (or hopes) might be interested in buying it.

If you decide to try direct mail then your first problem will be, of course, finding the names and addresses. There are several ways in which you can do this.

The first and cheapest is to compile your own list. Every time you sell a book you should keep the name and address of the person who bought your book. You can either write the names and addresses down in a little notebook or you can store them on a computer. The former is pretty useless. The latter is very useful.

Once names and addresses are in a computer (assuming that they have been stored in a special program which allows you to use them) you can print out labels whenever you want. If you have a purpose built program you can print out the names and addresses of all the men living in Wales who have bought your book entitled *Rock Climbing In The Welsh Valleys*. You can then send them details of your new book entitled *More Rock Climbing In The Welsh Valleys*. If your brochure makes your book sound attractive, and you are selling it at a good price, your mailshot should be successful.

At Publishing House we now have well over 100,000 names and addresses in a special computer program which enables us to select different groups of people in different parts of the country for new mailshots. Most important of all, the program we use enables us to ensure that we do not send details of a book to people who have already bought it. (I regard computer software as generally inefficient and overpriced but this is one area of publishing where computers and software can be of some assistance.)

If you don't have names and addresses of your own then you can either compile a list (by going through directories in your local public library) or you can buy a ready made list. Buying a list of names will cost you anything between £100 and £400 a thousand. You can buy lists of names through list owners, list managers or list brokers. Numerous companies produce directories of the lists they have available.

You can probably buy a list of general practitioners over the age of 40 who enjoy holidays abroad. You can almost certainly buy a list of science teachers between the ages of 21 and 30. You can, in short, buy virtually any list you are ever likely to want or need. But you must always remember that the more you pay for your list the more books you will have to sell in order to make a profit.

Your second problem will be writing the letter to send to your prospective buyers. Here are some tips.

1. Don't worry about grammar. Your direct mail leaflet should be easy to read. You're not trying to win prizes or impress the English teacher. You're trying to communicate with people.

2. Make sure that your direct mail letter has a PS. An amazing four out of five readers will read the PS in your letter before they read anything else. So you must have a PS. The PS should summarise (very briefly) some key benefit or simply encourage the reader of your letter to respond. (As in: 'Don't forget: our solid gold guarantee means that you have absolutely nothing to lose and everything to gain by responding to this offer'.) If you can think of an excuse to put in a PPS then do so. I have seen selling letters with seven PSs (going all the way down to PPPPPPPS).

3. Tell a story in your letter. Write your selling letter as though you were writing to a friend to tell them about an exciting new discovery. Keep everything you write simple and easy to read. Avoid using big words which your readers may not understand. Avoid too many adjectives and (especially) adverbs. Try to make sure that there is plenty of action in your copy. Some of the best and liveliest writing in Britain today appears in tabloid newspapers. Read the tabloids and absorb a little of the writing style the best writers use.

4. Use testimonials and quotations.

5. Use colour in your letter. Print some headlines in a colour, for example.

6. You must sign every letter. But you don't have to sit there and sign thousands and thousands of letters. Give the printer a copy of your signature and ask him to add to the end of every letter. And print your signature in a different colour to the copy of the text so that it stands out. Blue is a good colour for a signature.

7. Make sure that you indent the first line of every paragraph but don't always justify the right hand side of the text. Unjustified text (a ragged edge down the right hand side) can be easier to read and friendlier.

8. Use capital letters only occasionally. If you want to draw attention to a piece of text use bold or underline the copy. Capital letters look as though you are shout-

ing and making too much of an effort. In headlines you should use upper case for the first letters of key words only. Find the hottest benefit to the reader on each page in a leaflet and draw attention to that benefit in a headline. Put quotation marks around your headlines to make them more noticeable and memorable.

9. Whenever appropriate and possible use lots of facts and figures to substantiate any claims you make. Draw attention to these facts with bullet points down the left hand side of the text.

10. Use photographs and graphics wherever possible to liven up your pages. There should be a photograph of you (or the author if you aren't the author) and you should also reproduce your book cover. Remember that every photograph of an individual should be accompanied by a caption. So, if you have a photograph of yourself put your name under the photograph. You might like to add a quote if you can find one that seems suitable. (So, for example, if your name is Walter Wallkarpet and you have written a book on floor coverings and you were described by *Rug Weekly* as 'Britain's best known and most knowledgeable carpet expert' you might like to put this quote (attributed) under your name.)

11. Make sure that your leaflet is legible. Don't skimp on the ink. Your response will be around 10% higher if your printer uses lots of black ink. But your leaflet doesn't have to be expensively printed. Our least successful leaflet was packed with colour and printed on art paper – it did not do anywhere near as well as a leaflet containing the same information which was printed in black on fairly cheap paper.

12. Don't use full stops on headlines. You want your readers to keep reading. A full stop is likely to halt them in their tracks. And to keep people reading your leaflet make sure that you break the last sentence on every page of your sales letters. Just below the last sentence print: 'Please turn to page 2' (etc.).

13. You must print a code on all your leaflets so that you know which mailshot produced which response. If you have a coupon on your direct mail leaflet then you can get the printer to print identification codes on different batches of the same leaflet. Before the leaflets are printed you calculate how many you need with each particular code.

4. YOU MUST HAVE CONFIDENCE IN WHAT YOU ARE SELLING

You yourself simply must know why whatever it is that you are selling is the best. And you must have confidence. Self belief plays a large role in success. This is true whether you are selling door knobs, motor cars, surgical skills, house building expertise or lawn mowing know how. You must not allow your potential customer even to think of finding an alternative. There must be no alternative. Your customers simply must have your product. Your service or product must be unique. (You can help yourself identify the sort of 'uniqueness' which produces success by looking around the world and identifying successful products and individuals. Once you have done this ask yourself what it is about those products and individuals which makes them so successful.)

What previously undervalued, unmentioned skills and advantages can you offer? Why should customers deal with you? What are you good at? What are the obvious – and not so obvious – benefits of their developing a relationship with you?

You must decide what is special about the book you are selling – and the way you are selling it. Obviously, if you are selling through the mail then one big advantage you have to offer is that your customers don't have to catch a bus or drive into their nearest town and try to park. They don't have to go into a bookshop, look through all the dross laid out on the display tables, queue and then wait to order a decent book from you. Their book purchase from you comes post free and is guaranteed. If they want to send it back they get a full refund. What have they got to lose? Once you have isolated the advantage to the customer of doing business with you then you must tell – and remind – the customer of this advantage.

You must have confidence in what you are selling. If you do not admire the service or product you are selling – and genuinely believe that it is the best available – then your potential customers won't have faith either.

A Venetian nobleman once complained when a sculptor wanted to charge a hefty fee for a piece of work that was going to take ten days to create. 'You forget,' said the sculptor, 'that I have been thirty years learning to make that bust in ten days.'

Do not make the mistake of believing that you have to start with lots of money in order to make money. You don't. You can make a fortune without having much to start with. You need a little seed capital but your main requirements are ideas, enthusiasm, ambition and self belief. Ideas are power. And poverty and riches are both the result of faith.

'He's lucky,' people say. 'Everything he touches turns to gold.'

They say this, often with rather more than a tinge of envy, about anyone who has been able to make more than one business venture succeed. Most people never even try, let alone make, one venture succeed – and so they feel that anyone who is consistently or repeatedly successful must simply be lucky.

But luck has nothing (or, at least, very little) to do with business success.

Continued business success is a result of application, accuracy, attention to detail, planning, determination and reliability. Honesty, although not essential, is also pretty useful.

It was Burke who said, in the House of Commons in London, that he knew statesmen who behaved like peddlers and merchants who acted like statesmen. Whatever you do with your life you should always aim to act like a statesman. You may be able to make a lot of money in a short time by being dishonest. But you will not stay in business for long. If you want to keep on publishing books – and keep on selling them – then you must be honest and honourable. There really is no other way. You must also be sincere, understanding and sympathetic to the needs of your readers.

And you should know that hard work alone is not necessarily the route to making money.

Never forget this simple, self obvious, truth: if hard work alone created wealth then on Friday evenings our factories and mines and office buildings would disgorge millionaires by the busload.

5. *YOU MUST KNOW YOUR CUSTOMERS*

You must know your customers and you must know what they really want and really need (realising, of course, that they themselves may not know what they really want or need). Only when you know what they want and need can you give it to them.

Remember that self interest is the world's most potent driving force.

Whatever it is that you are selling your customers want to know what is in it for them. No one (apart from relatives and friends) is going to buy your book in order to make you happy; they are going to buy your product or your service because they need what you have got to offer. They will give you their money because you can satisfy one or more of their needs. In order to succeed you must offer them a service or a product which satisfies their fears or needs.

When you know what your customers want, and you know how to provide them with what they want, then you will get what you want. You will obtain the financial reward you feel you deserve and with the financial reward will come the freedom you want.

Knowing what your customers want (even when they don't) is one of the things which will make you successful. You need to identify and then satisfy the non verbalised (and possibly unrecognised) requirements of your customers-to-be.

If, instead of saying: 'What's in this for me?' you say: 'How can I make life better for my future customers?' you will benefit enormously.

The most successful people are the ones who have understood what their customers want and need – and who are prepared to provide a better service at a lower cost (in terms of both effort and money).

6. SELLING YOUR BOOK

The first and most important thing to remember is that you must try to forget that you are selling books.

Most people don't buy books.

Whether the book you have to sell is about trains, flower arranging, an imaginary cricket team on tour, mountain climbing, embroidery, murder on the Orient Express, irritable bowel syndrome or growing dahlias you are either selling information and advice or you are selling entertainment or you are selling a gift.

The remainder shops are stacked to the ceiling with beautifully illustrated, expensively-produced books which were written and published by people who didn't understand that simple rule of publishing life.

If you try to persuade people to take out their credit cards or cheque books simply to buy a book on flower arranging, you will have a hard time.

So, if your name is Gertrude Bloom and you have just written a book on flower arranging how can you persuade a complete stranger (even someone who is enthusiastic about flower arranging) that they must buy a copy of Gertrude Bloom's *Complete Book of Flower Arranging*?

You have two primary choices (and the choice you make will, of course, depend upon the content of the book).

First, you can decide that you are basically going to sell advice and information.

You can tell potential purchasers that your book on flower arranging will tell them everything they are ever likely to want to know about the subject. You can explain that your book will tell them precisely what to do to produce a stunning arrangement. You can tell them that 'the author has won prizes on three continents for her flower arranging skills'. And all that will help to sell your book.

But if you are going to make your book about flower arranging a real best seller you must understand what it is that your potential customers really want and need.

Now I know nothing whatsoever about flower arrangers or flower arranging but it is a pretty safe bet that most people who spend time, effort and money arranging flowers do so to please, impress and delight other people. If they arrange flowers professionally then they want their customers to be so thrilled that they rush and tell all their friends. If they arrange flowers for their own home then they will want to delight and impress their relatives and friends.

So, that is what you have to sell your potential customers: the prospect that they will, if they read your book, learn all the secrets about successful flower arranging and acquire astounding flower arranging skills. If they buy this book then they will impress and delight everyone who sees their work.

If you want to sell your book through the mail by using newspaper advertisements, or through a leaflet which you deliver to potential customers, then you have to make sure that the advertisement or the leaflet define and draw attention to these advantages.

If you intend to sell your book through bookshops then you must make sure that the cover of your book tells potential customers exactly how they will benefit if they buy your book. It really isn't enough to draw attention to your skills and achievements. You must make it clear that the purchaser of the book will, by having access to your advice and information, become just as skilful and successful as she or he would like to become.

The bottom line is that if you are going to sell a non fiction book successfully on the basis of the advice or information it contains then you have to remember that you are primarily selling dreams.

Your purchaser has a dream (which you may have helped arouse through your advertising) and your book is designed to help them satisfy that dream.

Your second chance of selling your book on flower arranging is to sell it as entertainment.

The book may, for example, contain very few practical tips and hardly any useful secrets that will help the reader become a better flower arranger.

But it may be stuffed from cover to cover with your excruciatingly funny anecdotes about flower arranging. There may be page after page detailing your side splitting experiences with fern, gladioli and chrysanthemums. You may spill the beans about behind the scenes experiences among the world's top flower arrangers.

The book may, in short, be an exciting, enthralling and irresistible read for anyone interested in flower arranging.

Sadly, however, there is a snag here which may interfere with your sales. If you have printed a relatively small number of books your unit price may have to be higher than the average flower arranger will want to spend on entertaining him or herself.

For example, you may have decided to test the market by printing just 1,000 copies of the book. You cannot sell the book for less than £9.95.

And many of your potential customers will regard that as too high a price to pay for a few hours' entertainment.

Your problem is that large, general publishers, bookshops and remainder shops – where books are routinely sold very cheaply – have devalued books and many consumers who would be happy to spend £9.95 on a CD or cassette tape, on a meal in a restaurant or on a theatre ticket, regard £9.95 as too much to spend on a book for themselves (despite the fact that they will obtain several hours of entertainment out of the book even if they only read it once).

So, do you give up?

Of course not.

Even though you know that many flower arrangers would love to read your delightful memoirs, you do not bother advertising the book to them directly.

Instead you advertise it to their friends and relatives. And you advertise the book as a gift.

Amazingly, there are thousands of people who have spent their lives in publishing and bookselling who still don't realise it but most of the books which are sold are sold as gifts. Ask any bookshop manager when he sells most books and he will tell you that he moves most of his stock – and makes most of his profit – in October, November and December. Sadly, some of the people who work in bookshops aren't too bright. Your idiot bookshop manager probably doesn't realise that he isn't selling books – he is selling·Christmas presents.

It is, of course, far easier to sell a book for £9.95 if you sell it as a gift ('The Perfect Present For Any Flower Arranger') but if you decide to sell your book this way you may decide to print it not in a paperback edition but in a hardback version. The reason for this is simple. A hardback book makes a better and more 'special' present than a paperback book. It seems more valuable and makes a more impressive gift.

Naturally, since you are selling a hardback book you can increase the price to cover the increased costs. As a publisher concerned with making a profit you will, of course, increase the price by slightly more than the increased unit cost of printing a hardback book.

7. *Promoting your book*

Once you have written (or had written for you) and published a book you have to promote it. I know that the idea of talking or writing about a book seems rather tacky and slightly distasteful but it is, nevertheless an inescapable part of the process.

It would, I know, be very nice if we could all write books and then sit back and wait for people to clamour for them. It would be wonderful if we could shyly push our books out into the world and then allow them to find their own readers.

Sadly, however, it doesn't happen like that.

Every year tens of thousands of brand-new books are launched. Add those to the hundreds of thousands of backlist books in existence and you will see that no book will stand a chance of finding any readers if it isn't promoted.

There are two basic ways of promoting a book.

The first is to rely on free advertising such as may be obtained through reviews, interviews, profiles, feature articles, book serialisations and so on.

The second is to rely on advertising which is paid for with hard cash.

There are advantages and disadvantages to both these types of advertising.

And do make sure that you send details of your book to Whitaker's British Books In Print. Whitaker's will list your book on their database. This is done free of charge and will enable literate staff in bookshops to find details of your book if a customer asks for it.

8. ADVERTISING YOU CAN GET FOR FREE

I am constantly amazed at the number of publishers who fail to take advantage of all the free advertising that there is around.

For example, a surprising number of publishers produce books which have absolutely nothing on the back cover. What an absurd waste of space this is. Watch people in a bookshop and you will see that the back cover is one of the first places they look. You can use this prime site in a number of ways. You can use it to promote the author in some way (with quotes, reviews and a picture for example). You can use it to promote other books you have published. Or, you can simply use the back cover to promote the book itself. If you have reviews or quotes use them. If you don't have any reviews or quotes then don't make any up (once you lose credibility no one will ever believe you again). Instead pick out sentences or paragraphs from the book which give potential readers a flavour of what to expect. Sometimes quotes from within the book are more powerful than reviews or reader testimonials.

Next, you should, whenever it is possible and appropriate, put advertisements in the back of your book. Publishers always used to do this but these days they don't bother. They either bind in lots of blank pages (what a waste that is) or else they simply throw away the pages they don't need for the book text (another waste). We always use every available page (that would otherwise be blank) to promote books on our backlist.

***

There are lots of other ways to get free advertising.

If you write an article for a newspaper or a magazine make sure that you ask the editor to allow you to mention your book at the end of your article. The article you write doesn't necessarily have to have anything to do with the book you have written. You are the link. Most editors will be happy to mention that you are the author of a book because this gives their publication a little extra touch of class. It is only a short step from getting a 'plug' for your book to 'selling off the page' by including details of how your book can be obtained by post.

(If you do this don't forget to include the price of the book, details of how cheques and postal orders should be made out and the address to which orders should be sent.)

And if you write a column for a newspaper or a magazine put a clause into your contract allowing you to sell your book(s) to your readers.

Obtaining publicity in your local newspaper and on your local radio and television stations should not be too difficult. Simply send them an advance copy of your book together with a press release explaining that you live in their catchment area. You may have to follow up with a telephone call but the chances are good that they will chase after you.

Here I think a warning about television might help. Many television presenters seem to think that there is something distinctly tacky and unprofessional about allowing an author to mention the title and/or publisher of his book. Prior to arriving at the TV studios you may be spoken to on the telephone by an exceedingly unctuous but at the same time pretentious creature (traditionally female but these days more commonly male) who will give the impression of being in charge of the whole TV programme and, indeed, quite a number of other important programmes. This person, who will turn out to be an assistant temporary junior researcher-cum-meeter-and-greeter at the TV station, will tell you that you will not be allowed to mention your book on air because of the station's policy. Pointing out that the station constantly carries paid for advertisements or (if it is the BBC) promotions for its own products will get you nowhere. There are several ways around this problem. If the programme is live then you can mention the title (and any other details which seem appropriate) as many times as you like before you are thrown off the programme and ejected from the studio by a puce faced producer. If the programme is recorded then I suggest you wait until about three minutes before the recording is due to start and then ask the producer to confirm that your book will be given a plug, either by the presenter or by you. If there seems to be any reluctance to mention your book you should ask about a fee. The producer will probably mutter something about paying your expenses. You should talk about your qualifications and professional expertise and suggest that a fee of £750 would be appropriate. Ask where you should send the bill. You will probably find that the reluctance to mention your book will suddenly and mysteriously disappear.

Having your photograph and a small feature on page 35 of your local newspaper will be a start. And a two minute spot on the local TV news will make you something of a temporary celebrity in the shops you visit regularly.

But, sadly, I must warn you that local publicity is not likely to sell too many books. To sell books you're going to have to pay for advertising.

9. ADVERTISING YOU HAVE TO PAY FOR

Free advertising can help you move a few books but unless you're very lucky (and there is always a large element of luck involved when you're trying to get free advertising since so many other factors can interfere with the amount of space you get) you aren't going to get rid of your print run with free advertising.

You are, after all, going to have to face the fact that the bookshops are unlikely to stock your new book in decent quantities. Many and possibly most of your books are going to have to be sold through the mail. You are, I am afraid, going to have to become a mail order publisher.

(If your primary motive in writing is to sell books, change the world, make some money, influence people and have fun then you won't mind this at all. After all, it really doesn't matter whether you sell your books through a bookshop or through the mail. What matters is that you sell books.)

Of course, before you start buying advertising space you have to have an advertisement. You have to have something to put in the piece of space you've bought.

When writing your advertisement remember that you must first of all grab the reader's attention. You must then interest him in your book. Then you have to get him to want to buy your book. And finally you have to make sure that he acts – and that you turn his attention, interest and desire into action. For more advice on how to write an advertisement that works see the section entitled 'Tips For Writing Ads That Work'.

Mail order specialists writing advertisements always look at everyone else's advertisements. They look because they know that the best way to learn how to write an advert is to look at what other people are doing. They don't copy other people's advertisements (that would be crude and it wouldn't work) but they do learn from them.

The big problem any mail order businessman (or businesswoman) faces when looking at advertisements is the fact that they don't know which advertisements make a profit and which ones make a loss.

So, to make life easy for you I'll tell you a secret that is worth several hundred times the cost of this book: the advertisements which are working are usually those which appear repeatedly. If you've seen an ad appear one hundred times over the last few years the chances are good that it is making money.

Any decent writer can write good advertising copy.

It requires different skills to writing a book or an article or a short story or a column.

But if you can write then it is a skill that can be learned.

I suggest that you write and prepare your advertisements yourself. You will probably do much better than if you hire an agency to write your copy. They will never understand your book as well as you will. And they will never care as much about its success. Worse still, advertising agents have a tendency to try to produce 'clever' ads which win prizes. Prize-winning ads don't usually sell anything. (Just as books which win awards are invariably unreadable and buildings which win prizes are often cold, unfriendly and impractical.) If your advertisements start winning prizes then I suggest you fire your advertising agency before you go bankrupt.

Do not worry about your advertisement or leaflet offending someone. If it doesn't offend someone then it probably won't work. Provocative advertising (like any good writing) makes people think – and that is exactly what you want it to do.

***

The single most important thing you must remember when buying advertising space is that you should hardly ever pay 'rate card'. Not paying 'rate card' when buying advertising is almost certainly the second most important factor which will decide whether your publishing venture is a success. (The first most important factor is, of course, the ability to write or commission a good, readable book that people enjoy reading. If you can't write or commission a good book then your publishing venture won't work because you will either fail to sell enough books to make a profit or you will find that the people who do buy books from you will be sending them back so fast that you will spend all your time writing out refund cheques.)

'Rate card' is the price that the publishers of magazines and newspapers say they want to be paid when they sell their advertising space. 'Rate card' is what big, rich advertisers (banks, insurance companies, car companies etc.) pay when they buy advertising.

Advertising comes in two prices: rate card and the price you are prepared to pay. You do not want to pay 'rate card'.

In one recent year we bought £492,000 worth of advertising (plus VAT). But to get nearly half a million pounds worth of advertising we had spent just £131,407 (plus VAT.). To save me doing the sums our advertising agency told me that this represented an average discount of 73% off rate card.

How did we do this? (This secret alone is worth a thousand times the price of this book).

We bought 'short term'.

What that means is that we bought most of our advertisements at the very last minute – we bought the left over space that the advertising sales people hadn't been able to sell and that would have remained empty if we hadn't bought it. Buying short term is a sort of charity work. We like to think that by agreeing to pay £800 for £4,000 worth of advertising space we are performing a public service.

You want to mop up the advertising space that no one else wants. You want to buy jumble sale price advertising. You want the advertising space that is left over at the end of the day and likely to go to waste if you don't buy it.

If a daily newspaper hasn't sold a chunk of space by 6.0 pm in the evening then they get very worried. That space will never come round again. They only print to-morrow's newspaper once. And if they don't sell the space in tomorrow's newspaper now then they will never sell it.

And so they will sell it to you for a fraction of the price that they would have sold it to you if you'd wanted to buy it a week ago.

Buying cheap, left over advertising space is known, in the trade, as buying 'short term'. And virtually every magazine and every newspaper in the entire universe will sell short term (though many of them will deny it). Posh newspapers sell 'short term'. Posh magazines sell 'short term'. No newspaper or magazine publisher likes having to put a charity ad onto money earning space. No newspaper or magazine publisher likes having to run one of those public service ads that they always keep in readiness for such a calamity. No newspaper or magazine publisher likes having to run an advertisement for another product in their own group. It is an insult to the advertising director and embarrassing to the publisher. They would much, much rather buy a real live advertisement from you and get some money (albeit you will be paying at a fraction of the price that the big name advertisers will buy space) to put in the bank.

'Short term' advertising space is the saviour of the mail order publisher. It is common to buy space at between a quarter and a third of the rate card price. I have, on occasion, bought advertising space at less than 10% of the rate card price. Only very large, stupid corporations pay the asking price for advertising space.

With magazines buying 'short term' often means buying space the day the magazine is due to be printed. And with newspapers, short term space is often sold just a matter of minutes before the presses start to roll (or jiggle backwards and forwards or whatever it is that they do these days).

If you want to do this (and it is, as you can imagine, an absolutely crucial part of the whole publishing process since the savings can, as I have shown, be phenomenal) then you have to have your advertisements ready and waiting. If you are buying short term you don't have time to design an advertisement or get it set, printed and prepared. It has to be ready to go. And, ideally, it should be sitting in the newspaper or magazine office's files, ready to be used.

***

Once you have created an advertisement and you are ready to start advertising you should always remember that by changing one small part of an advertisement you may be able to improve your response rate considerably. You might, for example, obtain a better response by moving or changing the headline, by altering the price or by offering a free gift. One of the reasons why it is vital to keep good records – showing the number of orders generated by every advertisement – is that it is only by keeping such records that it is possible to evaluate advertisements and compare each new advertisement with its predecessors.

It may take you a little while to find the right advertisement for your book – and the right place to advertise. (A good tip when deciding where to advertise is to look through a magazine or newspaper and see whether it carries any advertisements for books like yours – or for books at all. Then check to see if the advertisement appears again. If an advertisement appears more than twice in the same publication then it is a fairly safe bet that the advertiser is making money.)

When you start advertising in magazines and/or newspapers you will straight away have to choose between 'display' advertising and 'classified' advertising. The term 'classified' advertising describes those pages of the periodical (usually at the back) which include lots of small adverts (often for garden produce, rotary nasal hair clippers, loans and soft porn magazines or video tapes). In contrast the term 'display' advertising refers to the bigger advertisements (usually at the front) placed by larger companies (such as life insurance companies, banks, motor car companies and so on).

'Classified' advertising is usually cheaper than 'display' advertising (even if you buy the same sized piece of space) but you pay an extra price for that usually modest economy: in our experience it doesn't seem to work as well. Steer clear of classified advertising if you can and buy the same sized space in display advertising.

Don't expect to make a profit with your very first advertisement. But you will be extremely unlikely not to make *any* money out of an advertisement and since your overheads are likely to be low (and much lower than the overheads of a conventional publisher with smart offices in London and the salaries of a regiment of marketing men to pay) you should be able to keep your losses to a minimum.

You have to advertise at the right time. Generally speaking most mail order specialists claim that the best months for advertising are January, February, March, September, October and November. The next best months are April, May and June. The worst months for mail order advertising are July, August and December. It is also widely believed that advertising on or around bank holidays is commercially dangerous. Our experience does not support these general rules.

If you can buy advertising space cheaply enough then July and August can be very profitable months for mail order sales. And though I would not try general direct mail marketing through the post during those months I might try direct mail to the over 50s in the summer on the grounds that it is people with children who are usually away from home then – and most likely to throw away 'junk' mail when they come back home and find the stuff littering their hallway.

Bank holidays aren't necessarily a dead loss either. The success of an advertisement on a bank holiday seems to depend entirely on the weather. If you are a gambler or a weather forecaster then you might like to buy a cheap advertisement on a bank holiday. If it rains then people will stay in and read the papers. And there is a chance that your advertisement could do very well.

(I should perhaps point out that with any newspaper advertisement there is always a danger that a big news story might destroy your hopes. If an eminent member of the royal family dies on the day when you have an advertisement running then you will, I fear, almost certainly lose most of your money. This risk is there whether you are buying short term or not.)

If you get a choice choose advertising space in the first half of a newspaper or magazine (called, curiously, the 'book' in the business). Ask for an 'early' page. A right hand page will usually work better than a left hand page. And if you have a small advertisement try to be near the outside edge of the page rather than near the gutter (where the binding or staples are). If your advertisement has a coupon then the coupon needs to be near an outside edge so that buyers can reach it easily with their scissors.

If your advertisement isn't clearly printed or isn't in the position you agreed complain to the advertising department. If the error is a big one you can choose not to pay or to have the advertisement re-run. If the error is a small one you can ask for a reduction in the price.

***

And don't be afraid to ask for additional discounts. As a publisher you will be offering an advertisement that most publications will enjoy having on their pages. They would much rather have your ad than an ad for loans, soft porn telephone lines or sanitary protection. You help to give their publication gravitas. Take advantage of this and ask for an additional discount. If you do not use an agent when booking space ask the publication to give you the agency commission. This will usually be 15%.

Very large companies will sometimes do amazingly stupid things when buying space. This is because they have far more money than sense. For example, a company which is testing a new product may decide that it wants to buy advertisements only in the editions of a national newspaper which are sold in the South West of England. The agent may pay full price for this advertisement. (Why should they care? The size of their commission depends upon the size of the bill.) The result of this wastefulness is that the newspaper has to find an advertiser prepared to buy the same space in all the other editions of his newspaper. Big, important companies may consider it beneath them to mop up this advertising left over. You will not. You will offer a ridiculously small amount of money for the space and get virtually national advertising extremely cheaply.

You may find that you can buy advertising space at below rate card by approaching newspapers and magazines direct. But you will probably find it easier to buy space through a 'media buyer' who will act as an agent between you and a variety of publications. The media buyer will cost you nothing. He will receive a commission from the publications in which you buy space.

As with direct mail leaflets you must make sure that each advertisement you insert contains a code – preferably in the address to which readers reply. So, for example, you might invite readers who want to buy your book from your first advertisement in *The Daily Telegraph* to write to Dept DT1 whereas you might invite readers responding to an advertisement in *The Guardian* to write to Dept G1. Putting codes on your advertisements is vital. Without codes you won't be able to identify the sources of your orders – and you won't know which advertisements have worked and which have not.

It is vitally important that you keep a record for each advertisement – so that you can tell whether or not it was profitable.

If you don't do this there is a real risk that you will continue to buy advertising that is losing you money.

We use an ordinary spreadsheet so that we can see at a glance whether or not an advertisement is working.

The two basic costs are, of course, the cost of the advertisement itself (you can, if you like, add on the cost of having the advertisement made – we don't bother to do this on the grounds that if the advertisement fails to make a profit then the cost of creating the advertisement itself isn't going to make any significant difference and if the advertisement does make a profit then the cost of having the advertisement created will, in the long run, turn out to be fairly negligible) and the cost of fulfilling the orders (this cost includes the cost of the book you sent out, the cost of the padded bag, the cost of the postage, the cost of the label, the cost of putting the cheque into the bank, the cost of paying someone to open the orders, sort the cheques, and put books into padded bags and the cost of fulfilling the guarantee by sending back some money to unhappy, dissatisfied or fraudulent customers later on).

To obtain the cost of sending out books we usually divide the total income by the price of the book being sold and then multiply the number by the cost of the book, postage and so on.

We run different sets of spreadsheet entries for different books or offers.

This system enables you to work out how many books you would have to sell to make a profit. And it also enables you to work out how much you could pay for another advertisement – and hope to make a profit on that advertisement too.

If you keep a daily record of sales you will, after a few advertisements have appeared, be able to work out whether or not an advertisement is going to work after it has been running for no more than a day or two.

So, for example, we have discovered that if we have an advertisement in a newspaper on a Sunday then our total income from that advert is likely to be between 5 and 6 times the amount of money we take on the Tuesday after the advertisement appeared.

Of the first 16 advertisements which we bought for my book *Relief from Irritable Bowel Syndrome* just six made a profit. The profit we made on those advertisements just about balanced the losses we made on the other advertisements which hadn't worked. We were able to continue advertising the book because the profits were balancing the losses. But, of the second 16 advertisements we placed, 14 made a profit. We tinkered with the advertisements. We tried different magazines and newspapers. And we gradually bought advertising space at lower and lower prices.

We have since then noticed a similar pattern with other advertisement campaigns. Generally speaking our first advertisements begin by losing a little money or breaking even. But as we tinker with the advertisements and eliminate the magazines and newspapers which don't work we begin to make a profit.

Experienced mail order specialists claim that they aim to get a minimum of double their advertising money back in gross income. In other words if they pay £1,000 for an advertisement they want to sell at least £2,000 worth of books. That is a fine aim.

But as long as you avoid the temptation to buy large office blocks in expensive parts of large cities (a temptation which most large publishers do not seem able to resist) you can probably get by with a slightly lower return than this.

However, if you have a good product and you manage to buy a cheap advertisement you may be able to get a five fold gross return on your money – or even more.

10. INSERTS

When you buy a magazine do you routinely lift it up by the spine, shake out all the loose inserts and throw them away without even looking at them?

Each one of those oh-so-easily abandoned inserts represents an expectation of success, a wild hope, or even a desperate dream for the mail order businessman who had the inserts printed and paid for them to be stuffed into the magazine.

There are three basic costs in buying inserts.

The first cost is in designing and printing the insert itself. Since you will normally need to print at least 10,000 leaflets the cost of inserts is clearly quite high. You can cut the cost of printing leaflets by printing in huge quantities (for example, 100,000 leaflets). Printing in advance is a good idea if you think you might want to put inserts into magazines right at the last minute (when you will be more likely to be able to get a good price).

The second cost is the amount of money you have to pay to the owners of the magazine to persuade them to put your insert into their periodical. This fee will be quoted as a cost per 1,000 and you should be able to get the price down quite a way from the original, quoted price. Only large companies with more money than sense (and advertising agencies keen to maximise their own income by paying rate card prices) pay the asking price. Generally speaking, don't pay much more than £20 a thousand to put loose inserts into a magazine. If you do then the chances are that you will lose money. As with display and classified advertising the cost of buying the right to put your inserts into a magazine will be lower if you buy the right at the very last minute. But to do this you will have to have your inserts ready and waiting to be sent to the magazine's printers.

The third cost is the cost of shipping the leaflets from your printer to the magazine's printers. Don't ignore or underestimate this cost. You will be moving leaflets in fairly large quantities. That costs money – especially if you need to use a priority, 'last minute' despatch service.

When negotiating the insert deal ask the magazine (or their representative) how many loose inserts the magazine allows per issue. Three is fine, four or five is OK but if the magazine allows more than five loose inserts then I suggest you look somewhere else. I fear that when a magazine greedily stuffs itself full of loose inserts there is a danger that the reader may not look at any of them.

If you are thinking of selling your book through inserts then your first task is to start collecting, reading and studying the loose inserts you might normally throw away when buying a magazine. The best way to learn how to write and prepare an insert is to look at as many inserts as you can. (But you can make inserts work without spending a fortune on glossy, colour leaflets. We usually print in black on tinted paper inserts.)

11. THE TWO STAGE SELL

Most off the page advertising relies upon the customer seeing the advertisement, being attracted by the offer, cutting out a coupon (or writing a short letter), writing a cheque, putting the coupon and the cheque into an envelope and posting both items off to the advertiser. If the advertiser takes orders by telephone this process can, of course, be made considerably easier.

However, some advertising relies on what is called a 'two stage sell'. Here, the advertisement which appears on the page in the newspaper or magazine merely invites readers to write in for more information or for a free brochure or booklet. The respondent may be required to pay a small charge towards the cost of postage and packing, though sometimes this charge may be allowed against any future purchase.

Naturally, the advertiser hopes that when the potential customer sees the brochure or booklet which they have been sent they will want to buy whatever it is that is being advertised. The big advantage to the advertiser is that in a brochure or booklet he can put far more information (and therefore sell his product that much more effectively) than he could possibly cram into an advertisement in a newspaper or magazine without buying acres of space and spending an absolute fortune.

12. TIPS FOR WRITING ADS THAT WORK

1. You must know who is going to buy your book.

You must know exactly who you are aiming at. When you first start selling your book you will have to rely more on instinct than anything else. Who do you think is most likely to buy your book? If the book is about trains then it is a fair bet that people who like trains will want to buy your book. If you've written a science fiction novel then you are probably safe in assuming that people who read science fiction will be your best customers. If you've written a romantic novel then you will probably do better advertising your book to women than to men. As you begin to sell books so you will learn more and more about your readers/customers. As the months go by try to build up a profile of your average customer. Male or female? Young or old? The information you collect will enable you to target your advertisements more accurately – both in terms of the form they take and the words you use and in choosing the right places to put your advertisements.

2. Decide why should people buy from you

Tens of thousands of books are published every year. What makes your book special? Why should someone buy your book in preference to any other book? If you don't know exactly what it is you have to offer that makes you and your book unique then potential readers won't know either. A money back guarantee – though essential – doesn't make you special. Nor does 'free postage and packing'. You have to be able to offer readers something that no one else can offer them. And you must remember that although you may be able to sell a few books to friends and relatives simply because they know you and want to help you, people out there in the real world won't buy your book because they feel sorry for you or because they want you to succeed as a self publisher. Remember that would-be customers want to know what is in it for them if they buy your book. When writing an advertisement you must put yourself in the shoes of your potential customers. Your customers aren't interested in the fact that you have published your book instead of buying a new car. They don't care about the fact that you stayed up nights to complete the book. They will not be encouraged to buy your book by the fact that it is beautifully bound, or stored in a centrally heated bedroom or even by the knowledge that if you don't sell lots of books you are going to have to stick with the job at the bank until you retire. Many advertisers make the mistake of trying to sell themselves or their company when writing their adverts. They show a picture of their smart new factory or their fleet of vans because they are proud of what they have achieved. But none of this is of any interest or benefit to the customer. People don't buy a video recorder because it is made in Japan and has a touch button patented recording programme. They buy a video recorder so that they can watch programmes when they want to watch them rather than when they are broadcast (and because it enables them to avoid family rows by watching one programme and recording another). People don't buy a washing machine because it has seventeen programmes and is white and doesn't leak all over the floor. They buy a washing machine because it does the washing without a lot of backbreaking effort. People don't buy a novel because it took you three years to research. They buy a novel because they want to be entertained and because you have convinced them that your novel will entertain them. (Or they might buy it because they are looking for a suitable present for Uncle George and your advertisement has convinced them that your book is something he will love). Arthritis sufferers won't buy a book on arthritis because it is printed on acid free paper and contains 267 pages. But they will buy a book on arthritis which they believe will tell them how to deal with the pain and stiffness of their arthritis. Before you write your advertisement ask yourself what it is that your potential buyers really want – what will make them want to buy your book. How will people benefit by responding to your advertisement? In what way will their lives be better as a result of sending you their money? You must offer the reader a solution to a problem he might not even know he has. After you have written your advertisement read it again and see whether or not you think it will excite a potential customer enough to encourage him to give you his money for your book.

3. Don't try to be too clever.
Advertisers and advertising agencies who want to win prizes often produce wonderful looking adverts. But all the evidence suggests that clever, prize winning ads don't

usually sell the product. Big advertisers who rely on retail sales don't have a quick way of testing whether or not their ads have worked. And so they are likely to waste a great deal of money on ineffective advertising. Mail order advertisers, on the other hand, will know within a day or two of an ad appearing whether or not it is going to make money for them. So when you are planning your first ads take a look at the mail order ads rather than the fancy, clever, often incomprehensible ads. Mail order ads look the way they do because they work.

4. Your ad must be eye-catching

We are all constantly exposed to advertisements. We ignore most of them and train our eyes to slide past anything that doesn't truly grab us. If you are advertising in a newspaper or magazine you have just over a second to catch the reader's eye and so if your advertisement is going to work it must contain something (possibly a photograph but more commonly a headline) that is irresistible. A good, catchy headline should contain no more than 15 to 17 words and should make the reader want to know more. Your headline should make the reader curious and, ideally, at the same time promise the reader something he can't resist. An effective headline does not necessarily have to refer to the book you are selling but it should engage the reader's emotions and make him or her want to read more. For example, if you are selling a book aimed at back sufferers you might grab your reader with the simple two word headline 'Back Sufferers'. This would attract the reader's attention. And then, underneath this, you could add the three words 'Relief at last!'. This would, hopefully, ensure that he became interested and wanted to read on. Your task in the rest of your advertisement would be to turn his interest into a sale. If you are selling a book which you know will be bought as a Christmas present you could use the headline 'Your Christmas Present Problems Solved!' to attract would-be buyers to your advertisement. Incidentally, headlines seem to work better when they are put within quotation marks.

You should never forget that to a certain extent your success will be determined not by what you have to sell but by the way that you sell it. (If your book is good – and the people who buy it are happy with it – then your success as an author and publisher will be assured if you are successful at giving your book a start in life. Word of mouth recommendations will ensure that your books become popular. On the other hand if your advertisements are better than your book you will not succeed because you will find yourself dealing with lots of returns and many complaints.)

5. Your advertisement must be well-written.

Writing advertisements that sell books requires just as much skill as writing books that sell. If an advertisement is to work it must be well-written, convincing and easy to read. The text of the advertisement must maintain the interest triggered by the headline. You have to be careful with humour when writing an advertisement. Not every potential buyer has a good (or even any) sense of humour. And don't try to be too clever with sophisticated layouts or fancy type faces.

The aim of the headline on your advertisement is to get the reader to read the rest of the advertisement. That's all. You can sell your book in the 'body copy' of the advertisement but the job of the headline is to draw in the reader from all the other distractions on the same page. If your advertisement is not read then you definitely won't sell your book and your money will have been wasted. Here are some tips to help you write a good, effective headline:

1. Try to use the first or second person and the present tense.

2. Don't be afraid to write a long headline. (But don't use more than 17 words in a headline.)

3. Put the headline within quotation marks. An advertisement headline draws 28% more attention if it is within quotation marks. Headlines on advertisements and direct mail leaflets are as important as titles on books.

And now here are some tips for writing the advertisement itself:

1. When writing the body copy for your advertisement use the same sort of typeface that is normally used in editorial copy in that publication. You want readers to look at your headline and not be entirely sure whether they are looking at editorial or at an advertisement.

2. Begin your advertisement body copy with a drop letter. This will help draw the reader to your copy – and encourage him or her to start reading.

3. Don't put the price in big letters. There is plenty of time for readers to find out the price when they have read your advertising copy.

4. If you have a coupon in your advertisement (and most advertisers who sell by mail order believe that a coupon can be important) have a thin dotted line around it (with a small pair of scissors to show the reader what to do). Don't use a thick dotted line or else you will risk frightening off a potential customer.

5. Put a copyright notice at the bottom of your advertisement.

6. Don't be devastated if your advertisement doesn't work. As few as 20% of new mail order advertisements work. If your advertisement doesn't work try another headline or rewrite the body copy.

7. Don't forget to include the title of your book (and the price) together with your

address and telephone number on every page and every piece of mailing literature you send out. And if you publish an advertisement which contains a coupon repeat the details of where and how you can be reached outside the coupon. Just think how terrible it would be if you lost a customer who wanted to buy your book but couldn't because the coupon had already been clipped or the part of the leaflet containing your address had disappeared.

Some words have a magical effect when included in advertisements and I suggest you look carefully at the list of 49 magic words and phrases in the next section.

When you have written your advertisement (or your selling leaflet) go through it and try to eliminate the two words 'that' and 'then' from your copy. These two words are grossly overused. They weaken strong copy and waste space.

Read your advertisement out loud once you've written it. This will give you a chance to spot any ambiguities, errors or confusing statements. If you can find someone else to listen while you read out the ad that is even better! And remember that the ultimate sin is to write boring copy.

And, when writing an advertisement remember that the basic question asked by every customer is: 'What's in it for me?'

6. Use testimonials.

If all goes well you will, within a fairly short period of time, begin to receive lovely letters from some of the people who have bought your book. You can use extracts from these letters to help give your advertisements credibility. (Before you use names you must, of course, write and ask the letter writer for permission. If you simply use initials and the letter writer can't be identified then it probably isn't necessary to obtain permission.)

If you yourself are an expert and your book is about the subject of your expertise then you must establish your credibility in your advertisement. Give details of your qualifications, achievements and honours.

7. Don't go over the top.

Potential buyers simply won't believe you if you promise too much. If you announce that your novel is 'the greatest story ever written' you will lose credibility – and sales. Boast that your book will help people live to 150 years of age and readers will turn over the page and ignore the rest of your advertisement.

8. Make it easy for customers to buy your book.

You would be surprised how often mail order advertisements appear without the name and address of the seller. Your advertisement must include your name and address, the price of your book, whether there is any extra charge for postage, what guarantee you are offering, what purchasers should write on their cheque and, if there isn't a coupon to fill in, a reminder to them to include their name and address when they write to you. If you take orders by telephone and/or by credit card then you should obviously include a telephone number and details of which credit cards you take. If you take orders by fax then include the fax number. If telephone calls are answered by a real, live person during normal office hours then say so – and spell out your version of 'normal office hours'. You need your customers to give you their name and address and, if they are paying by credit card, their credit card details. You must tell them how long they are likely to have to wait for their book ('We aim to send out all books within 48 hours but please allow 28 days for delivery') or else customers will be ringing up after three days to accuse you of stealing their money and to complain that they haven't yet received their book.

13. MAGIC WORDS AND PHRASES

Here is a list of 49 magic words and phrases which can turn an advertisement into a success:

free	how	new	easy	complete
exclusive	original	you	now	breakthrough
win	buy	today	yes	make money
guarantee	learn	send for	find out	special offer
secrets	how to	learn	discount	how would
the best	save	success	power	the truth of
hurry	easy	amazing	quick	amazing facts
bargain	at last	advice	protect	announcing
life	sale	you too	love	claim your
do you	discover	bargain		

The two most powerful words in advertising are 'free' and 'you'.

14. HEADLINES THAT SELL BOOKS

Here are some advertisements which have worked:

❖ The Secret of Making People Like You

❖ Five Familiar Skin Troubles – Which Do You Want To Overcome?

❖ You Can Laugh At Money Worries If You Follow This Simple Plan

- ❖ How To Talk To Your Cat

- ❖ When Doctors Feel Rotten This Is What They Do

- ❖ Read And Make Money

- ❖ Do You Make These Mistakes In English?

- ❖ The Little Mistake That Cost A Farmer $3000 A Year

- ❖ Whoever Heard Of A Woman Losing Weight And Enjoying Three Delicious Meals At The Same Time?

- ❖ Discover The Fortune That Lies Hidden In Your Salary

- ❖ How I Improved My Memory In One Evening

- ❖ How I Made A Fortune From A Fool Idea

- ❖ Do You Do Any Of These 10 Embarrassing Things?

- ❖ Imagine Me...Holding An Audience Spellbound For 30 Minutes

15. *THE SINGLE SECRET THAT GUARANTEES SUCCESS*

In order to persuade people to part with their money – and give you their custom – you have to remove as much of their risk as you possibly can. You have to take the risk – instead of your customer having to take it. The more you remove the risk involved in their doing business with you the more likely they will be to buy your books.

People are becoming increasingly distrusting and fearful and apprehensive about making a commitment to purchase anything – whether it be a product or a service. Most people have been disappointed. They have bought products which failed to do everything the advertisements claimed. They have been ripped off.

Persuading complete strangers to send you their hard earned cash so that you, in turn, will send them a book requires a great deal of trust on their part. Most people have learnt to be suspicious, cautious, sceptical and cynical about advertisement promises. How do they know that your book will be as good as you have made it sound? How do they know that you won't just send them a few pages of badly printed rubbish? How do they know that you will send them anything at all? How do they know that you won't just cash their cheque and run off with their money.

Your book may sound much better than anything else they have ever heard of. It may sound much more attractive and useful than anything that is likely to be available in the local book store. And because you can do business over the telephone or through the mail you are certainly much more convenient than any bookstore could ever be.

But, inevitably, at the back of everyone's mind will be the fear that you are maybe just trying to rip them off. Even if that isn't a fear they will undoubtedly worry that your book might not live up to expectations. There is a very good chance that every one of your potential customers will have, at some time or another, been ripped off by someone. They may have been ripped off by another mail order advertiser.

Now, you don't want to rip them off. You are far more interested in a long term relationship with them than in making a small but immediate profit. You have made absolutely sure that the book you are offering lives up to all the promises in your advertisement. You are confident that when they see the book you are selling they will be pleased with it. You know that they will want to read it, keep it and, hopefully, recommend it to their friends. You believe that there is a good chance that they will be so pleased with the book you send them that they will order from you again, and become long term customers.

All your potential customers know that if they buy a book at a bookshop they can examine it carefully before they buy it. They can look at the contents list. They can read a few paragraphs at random if they want to. They can compare it with whatever else might be available. They can look at the quality of the paper and the binding.

But buying from you involves a risk.

And that risk may prevent them from ordering your book.

And so the simple answer is that in order to help them take the plunge and order your book you must remove all the risk from the transaction.

You will dramatically increase the amount of business you get by taking away the risk of doing business with you. If you give a formal guarantee you will dramatically increase your sales.

Somewhere on your advertisement you make it perfectly clear that if, when they have received your book and had a chance to look at it, study it and read it, they do not feel that it was worth the money then you will give them their money back.

Simple!

With just a few words you have removed the risk from the transaction for the potential customer.

The three most powerful words in publishing are 'Money Back Guarantee'.

Spell out exactly what you are promising to do (I suggest that you simply offer to refund the customer's money if, for any reason, he isn't happy with his purchase) and then make sure that you stick to your promise.

Publishing House offers a very simple and straightforward guarantee: if a purchaser of one of our books wants a refund then, as long as the book is returned within 28 days in saleable condition we return the customer's money. We make sure that refund cheques are sent out as a priority – customers who are unhappy for any reason don't have to wait for a month to get their money back. What could be simpler than that?

The longer your guarantee period the more people will like it. A 28 day guarantee will do better than a 21 day guarantee.

Removing the element of risk is particularly important if you are selling products by mail order – where the customer hasn't seen what you're selling and has to rely on your advertising literature. Providing a guarantee, and then sticking to it, is the best way I know of to build up a lifetime relationship with your customers.

By removing the risk you have immediately given yourself a massive advantage over ordinary publishers and high street bookshops.

Most of your potential purchasers know that if they buy a book from a bookshop they will have no chance at all of returning it for a refund if they subsequently discover that it isn't as good as they had hoped it would be.

But your guarantee means that they can even get their money back if they find another book they like better. They don't have to give a reason for returning the book and asking for a refund.

By promising your potential customers that if they don't like the product they buy from you then you will – without any fuss and without them having to explain why they don't like the book – give them a refund, you are immediately trumping all the advantages offered by the local neighbourhood bookshop.

Most important of all you are making it clear that you have total confidence in the book you are selling. And your confidence will be contagious.

We always draw attention to our guarantee because we think that removing the risk from the transaction is vital.

For example, on advertisements for my book called *Relief from Irritable Bowel Syndrome* we include the totally true phrase 'You have nothing to lose but your symptoms'.

The reader with IBS who sends us a cheque cannot lose. If the book is as good as we say it is then for just a few pounds he or she will have acquired valuable information about a life destroying problem. But if the book doesn't look good, and the advice doesn't sound convincing then the book can be sent back and a full refund obtained. There is no risk at all – but plenty of possible gain.

***

With a guarantee of this sort what sort of returns can you expect? Much less than you probably expect for most people will respond in an honest way. If you send them a book which they value they will be happy to keep it.

Most mail order publishers who offer a guarantee expect to receive about 5%

returns. In other words five out of every 100 buyers will return the book they have bought and ask for their money back. If your product isn't as good as people expect it to be, or if your customers feel that they have not received value for money, then you may get a much higher return rate than this. I know of one man in the mail order business who gave up and insisted that mail order operations were impossible after he consistently received between 60% and 70% returns.

Despite our solid gold guarantee our returns rate runs at about 1% – and that includes customers writing in to say that their book has been damaged in the post, hasn't arrived at all or is not the book they ordered. (Sometimes they ordered the wrong book by mistake. Sometimes we sent them the wrong book. It doesn't matter whose fault it is we just send them the book they really want.) The bottom line is that we only send refund cheques to less than 1 in 100 customers. It is one of the lowest refund rates in the mail order business. I'm very proud of that.

It is a good idea to keep an eye on the level of your returns because the number of returns you are getting will tell you how good a service or product you are providing. And if you want to be successful then you must provide a good service and product.

Mail order publishing really works best if many of the people who buy one book from you go on to buy a second, a third, a fourth and so on.

Try not to regard mail order returns as a hassle. Instead regard them as another selling opportunity. Send a cheque back within a day or two of getting the returned item and with the cheque enclose a letter of apology. It's also a good idea to enclose a voucher that can be used against some other item in your catalogue.

The customer who gets his refund quickly and painlessly will trust you. He or she now knows that your guarantee is as good as you say it is. He or she could become a good customer in the future.

16. Laws, Regulators and Regulations

We live in a heavily regulated world. If you want to cross the street you have to find a spot which has been marked as suitable for that purpose. If you want to park your motor car you have to find a regulated parking place and pay the appropriate fee. If you want to travel you have to stuff your pockets with paperwork and documents proving that you are who you say you are and showing that you have paid for the right to travel.

It is, therefore, hardly surprising that if you want to publish and sell your own book you will have to deal with a variety of regulators.

You may feel that it is only fair that there should be some rules. After all, if there weren't any controls on publishing anyone would be free to write anything they liked about anyone else.

However, in our society the risk of an author saying unfair or unjustifiable things about someone (or some organisation or limited company) is restrained by the existence of our draconian and libel laws.

The libel laws are so biased against writers that there are those who regard them as, under some circumstances, to be allegedly and laughably unjust.

I do not intend to attempt to deal with the risk of libel in detail here. Men and women who spend their entire lives working with the libel laws often admit that this is an area of the law where good sense does not play a prominent role. 'In most areas of the law it is safe to say that in nine out of ten cases the outcome will satisfy the rules of common sense,' said one lawyer. 'But in the area of libel law these proportions are reversed.'

Anyone who writes a book takes a risk that he or she will be sued for libel. If the book is non fiction then the risk is that real people who are mentioned in the book (or who think that they are mentioned in the book) may jump up and down and claim that they have been libelled. If the book is a work of fiction then there is a risk that real people who have names similar or identical to characters in your book may suddenly appear and claim that you have deliberately libelled them and made an attempt to wreck their lives.

Naturally, in these circumstances, the plaintiff (or, if you are really unlucky, plaintiffs) will claim that the book has ruined their spotless reputation, damaged their ability to earn a living and ruined their social life. Such absurd exaggerations are necessary in order to win a damages jackpot.

(Our courts seem to regard emotional hurt as far more worth of financial recompense than physical hurt. Lose all four limbs and you may, if you prove that someone was responsible for your loss, be awarded a pittance. Convince a court that you have been hurt by allegations in print and you may be awarded a lottery jackpot sized win.)

You may think that if your book is published by a conventional publisher you will be protected by the publisher. But you should not put too much faith in this quaintly old-fashioned and comforting thought. These days most publishing contracts seem to contain a clause which puts all the responsibility into the pocket of the author.

Under some circumstances an author can be worse off if his book is published by a conventional publisher. These days there is a real risk that the publisher will settle with the plaintiff, paying his or her costs, handing over a small sum in damages and dumping all the responsibility on the author's doorstep. This may then leave the author alone, friendless and out in the open. Worse still it is not unheard of for a publisher to then demand that the author pay his costs, the costs that have been paid to the plaintiff and the damages that have been paid to the plaintiff. The beleaguered author can then find himself being attacked by lawyers acting for everyone.

The best solution is, I fear, to go through your book looking for potential litigation (and remembering that it is the words and phrases which seem most innocent and innocuous which, in the end, always seem to cause the greatest trouble). Read what you have written and ask yourself who might be offended by it.

If you are writing or publishing fiction then you should take all the precautions you can to ensure that you do not inadvertently libel someone you have never even heard of. For example, if you are writing a novel about a specific place and the book contains a character who is a crooked policeman it would be sensible to check with the local constabulary that there is no one of that name in the area. If you write a book which contains an evil doctor you should obviously take the elementary precaution of checking with the General Medical Council to make sure that they do not have someone of that name (or a similar name) on their lists of people licensed to practise medicine. You can also check with local telephone directories to reduce the risk of litigation. Keep a list of everything you have done to make sure that you do not libel someone accidentally. Your precautions may not prevent a lawsuit but they may help reduce the size of the damages a plaintiff is awarded.

***

You might think that the libel laws offer constraint enough to authors and publishers. But there are, of course, many other laws which regulate what you can and cannot put into a book.

If you write a non fiction book and include bad advice then you might be sued. For example, if you produce a cookery book which includes a recipe in which there is a mistake you might be sued by a reader who used your book and was made ill as a result of the error.

The number of ways in which an author can get into trouble simply by writing a book seems to grow every year. As with libel, all you can do is to use your common sense, do everything you can to ensure that your book is accurate and include the usual warning at the front of the book.

In a work of fiction it is customary to include at the front of the book a paragraph in which the author points out that the characters in his book are not based on nor intended to bear any resemblance to any living person. In a work of non fiction it is more appropriate to include a paragraph in which the author warns readers not to take any notice of any of the advice in his book.

17. Reviews

Strictly speaking I suppose that 'reviews' should be listed under the heading 'Free Advertising' but since a good deal of pompous nonsense is talked about book reviews I decided that reviews deserved a section of their own.

The first and most important thing to remember is that you should not expect your book to be widely reviewed. The chances are that if you publish it yourself then your book will be completely ignored – however good it is.

Newspapers and magazines which take books seriously enough to hire literary editors usually appoint vain, pseudo-intellectual nonentities who know virtually nothing about writing, books or publishing but who love going to literary parties and who bathe endlessly in their own (exclusively job derived) sense of self importance.

Literary editors (most of whom would dearly love to write books but cannot) show a natural aversion towards authors whose books sell in large quantities and much prefer to devote space to those authors whose books are unlikely to sell very well and whom they can, therefore, patronise endlessly.

My own experience is probably fairly commonplace: my first published books were widely reviewed in the national newspapers but the more successful I have become (and the more books I have sold) the rarer have become the reviews.

Most literary editors routinely dislike small, new publishing houses (and large, publishing houses which try to make a profit by producing books which there is a chance which people might want to read).

Some literary editors proudly announce to anyone who will listen that they steadfastly and automatically refuse even to consider books published by small publishers. Literary editors much prefer to review books by academic authors who neither hope nor expect to make any money out of their books. They try to ensure that most of their space goes to publishing houses which have well established reputations but which have long since lost all touch with reality and which employ editors who would much prefer to be involved with esoteric volumes which may create some sort of mild, obscure and unthreatening academic controversy (literary editors are, as a breed, very pro establishment and usually eschew risk and real controversy) but will never involve anything as vulgar as a reprint.

As a small publisher you must, I fear, accept that your book will probably not be reviewed in the national press. This is neither rational nor fair but it is the way it is. If this makes you feel angry and frustrated then you can, perhaps, take some small comfort from the knowledge that most literary editors live entirely on borrowed power. The power they have comes with the job. When they lose jobs (as most of them do every few years) they lose all their power.

Despite the fact that reviews will probably be as rare as smiling traffic wardens you will still want to do everything you can to get reviewed.

Send out review copies of your book at least 6 weeks before publication. (Unless you have written something so explosive that you need to keep it under wraps until publication date). You can enclose with your book a note asking for a copy of any review to be sent to you but this will almost certainly be ignored. If you want to save money you can send out a press release instead of a book – inviting literary editors to get in touch with you if they want a review copy. This may sound attractive but it will almost certainly result in silence.

You should compile your review list with some care. You may want to include national newspapers, (to say that getting a review in a national paper is something of a long shot is akin to saying that there may be rain in Britain at some time during the summer, but it will make you feel really good when or if it happens), large regional newspapers, specialist magazines and (if you are desperate for some sort of newspaper coverage) local newspapers.

If you know people working on newspapers it is usually considered part of the game to push your book onto them in the hope that they will give you a review. The London literary scene depends very much on this mutual back scratching among authors but since you and I will almost certainly be excluded from it (well, I am certainly excluded from it and I'm guessing that you will be too) we can look upon this inbred process with jaundiced, cynical and disapproving eyes.

If you have high hopes that your book will be widely reviewed and quoted and you suspect that you may not see all of these reviews and quotes then you should consider subscribing to a cuttings agency. This is not cheap, but it will dramatically improve your chances of seeing cuttings relating to you or your book. Since cuttings agencies usually search on one particular word or name I suggest that rather than registering the title of your book you give your own name. This will ensure that you don't have to keep on paying separate sums whenever you have another book out.

18. The importance of the free gift

You should remember that people usually need an inducement in order to persuade them to buy whatever it is that you are selling. The inducement must be something which people want. Ideally, you should give them something which is worth more to them than the product which they are buying! There is no point in offering a 'free' gift which no one wants. For example, a dentist who tries to persuade more patients to join his practice by offering free root canal surgery will probably be disappointed. How many people really want free root canal surgery? A year's free supply of specially approved toothpaste and toothbrushes, although unimaginative, might be a more successful inducement. Or, better still, a free high value book packed with practical tips on all aspects of health care.

What do you give away with a book? Well, another book is one real possibility. Or a booklet, perhaps. If you have written a book about motorways in the north of England you could give away a booklet describing all the service stations on those motorways. If you have written a book about walking in the West Country you could give away a booklet listing the twenty best pubs in the region.

An inducement is a bribe to buy. It should, ideally, be something that seems to have even greater value than the product you are selling. It must be something that the reader really wants. If you can give your customers something free which is (or seems to be) worth more to them than the product they are buying then your product will become irresistible.

Your aim may be to spread your message and try to change the world but you won't be able to do either of those things unless you first of all grab people's attention. You can't do any good at all unless people listen to what you have to say.

Finally, if you include a free gift with a book which is ordered and you will delight and surprise your customer. Not many people expect to find themselves doing business with someone who delivers more than they promise.

19. DESPATCHING YOUR BOOKS

It is possible to arrange a distribution deal with an established, orthodox publisher. You arrange to have your book set, printed and bound and then delivered to the 'proper' publisher. He will store and distribute your book with his own titles. Your book will be sold by his representatives and may even appear in his catalogue. You will be responsible for publicising and promoting your book. The snag, of course, is money. You will have to pay a handling charge of around 25% of the net receipts to the publisher for this service. And since you will also have to pay anything between 35% and 50% to bookshops and wholesalers there will not be very much left to cover your costs. If you take this route you will have to watch out for 'returns' from bookshops. If bookshops order and then later return vast quantities of your books you could still end up paying a commission on the sale of those books.

Alternatively, if you don't want to work with an orthodox publisher you can arrange for your books to be handled by a trade distributor who will provide warehousing space for storing your books and then make sure that your books are sent out to whichever bookshops order them. You will be responsible for making sure that bookshops order your books.

When you begin, and your publishing business is small, you can get away with buying a few sheets of stamps (the one organisation which will not give you any credit is the Post Office), an accurate set of parcel scales and a supply of padded bags. But if things go well it will not be long before you find that you need something more organised.

Publishing House is now big enough to be able to largely ignore stamps. Our outgoing mail is put into grey sacks and collected by the Royal Mail which then weighs the mail and takes appropriate sums from my bank account at regular intervals.

If we are doing a large scale mailshot we sort the mail by post code in-house. The Royal Mail sells us postage at a reduced rate to reflect the fact that we are doing some of their work for them. If you are doing a test mailing it is possible to obtain a special price for postage though you can only do this if you are sending out at least 4,000 items of mail.

If you don't have time to get involved in putting books in bags and dealing with cheques and customer orders you can hire someone to do all the day to day work for you. There are a number of fulfilment houses around which make their living dealing with orders and dispatching orders for mail order companies.

If you are dealing with the mail yourself then you should obtain copies of all Royal Mail leaflets which describe how to send parcels, packets and letters abroad. As far as postage is concerned we regard the world as consisting of three areas: UK, Europe and the rest of the world. We usually send books within the UK without any extra charge for postage or packing. We charge a small sum for postage and packing within the rest of Europe. And we charge slightly more for postage and packing to the rest of the world. Our aim is never to make money out of postage charges – but simply to cover our costs.

20. BUYING YOUR STATIONERY

When you begin you can simply obtain your stationery from a local stationery store. Easy. But when you start buying padded bags by the hundred (which you will do quite early on in your career as a publisher) you may find it easier to open an account with a supplier who will deliver to your door. You will almost certainly find it cheaper to buy stationery this way. (Although do be careful: the catalogues produced by mail order stationery companies are so inviting that it is very easy to order lots of things which look pretty and fun but which you do not really need.)

21. INSURANCE

If you work from home then you will need to make sure that you tell your insurance company exactly what you are doing. And once you take delivery of your first batch of books you will have to start insuring your stock. And, of course, if you employ people to help you with your publishing operation you will need to make sure that they are insured. If you carry insurance then the chances are that nothing will ever happen. If you do not carry any insurance then the chances are that someone hired to help you by carrying piles of books up and down the stairs will trip, fall and break a leg.

22. ORDERING REPRINTS

Ordering reprints has to be done well in advance. Printers are busier at some times of the year than at others. Ask your printer if he has any quiet times. You may be able to negotiate a special, low price if you can plan far enough ahead to be able to order your reprints at a time that is convenient to the printer. Unless paper prices have rocketed, or it is a long time since your first printing, or you are printing in very small quantities, you may find that reprinted books cost you slightly less than copies of the original book you are reprinting. This should enable you to make a slightly higher profit.

23. SALES REPRESENTATIVES

Early in my career as a publisher I hired some freelance sales representatives to sell my books into the bookshops. There are quite a few freelance sales representatives operating these days. The system works quite simply. The salesman will work on behalf of a number of small publishing houses which cannot afford to hire their own sales representatives. When the salesman arrives at a bookshop he will talk about all the books his clients are currently trying to sell (including their backlists).

When I had sales representatives the arrangement I had was that the representatives would receive a percentage of the sales made through the bookshops. However, I halted this arrangement quite early on in my career as a publisher and do not, at the moment, use sales representatives.

I had no problem with the sales force (who, in my view, did remarkably well in view of the fact that bookshops are generally resistant to small publishing houses). The difficulty I did encounter was the fact that because I was spending quite a lot of money on newspaper and magazine advertisements, and also sending out quite a number of mailshots, I knew that a number of the bookshop orders that were generated were inspired by my advertisements. I knew that even without salesmen I would sell some books to bookshops (these would be usually on a 'firm sale' basis since the bookshops were invariably ordering only because they were responding to customers orders – if your advertisements are effective many of the people who see them will go into bookshops to order your books, even though you offer to send the book post free) but it was impossible to differentiate between those orders which had been generated by the salesmen's visits to the bookshops and those which had been generated by my advertisements and mailshots. I knew that if I gave a commission to the salesmen on sales which had been triggered by my advertisements then I would soon be in trouble (since I was already paying for the advertisements!)

24. Staff

To begin with you may, if you have the time and the patience, be able to cope with everything that needs to be done by yourself. But as your publishing venture grows you will quickly find that you need help. This will, in part, be because there simply won't be enough hours in the day to put books into bags, deal with printers, book-shops and newspaper advertising departments, and get on with writing your next book. But it may also be because you will find that there are some aspects of publishing which you don't do as well (or enjoy as much) as the writing the books bit. Before you hire anyone talk to an expert about the relevant legislation. Being an employer means constantly facing new laws and dealing with seemingly endless regulations.

25. Should you charge for postage and packing?

Some mail order experts claim that people buying through the mail are blind to charges made for postage and packing and handling. You can, they say, add a postage, pack-ing and handling charge of £2.95 or £3.95 onto the price of a book without losing a single sale.

My experience is different. We tested this hypothesis in the most scientific way we know how. We printed several thousand catalogues which were identical apart from the fact that half of the catalogues offered books post free while the other half included a charge.

The result was very convincing. It seemed clear that the people who had re-ceived the catalogue with the extra charge for postage and packing were ordering fewer books than the people who had received the catalogue with books offered on a post free basis.

Since then we have not usually charged extra for postage and packing. (There are, of course, occasional exceptions. For example, if a book is particularly heavy then we may charge extra for postage. And if we are selling a book at a very low, giveaway price we may add a postage charge. We also charge extra for postage when sending books outside the UK.)

The advantage of charging extra for postage and packing is that if a customer returns a book you only have to send back the price he paid for the book. You can keep the 'postage and packing' element of the price.

26. YOU NEED AN ADDRESS WHERE ORDERS CAN BE SENT

Think very carefully about the address you are going to use. If you use your home address then the chances are that you will have readers calling in for tea. That might be very pleasant (depending, of course, upon the reader) but you will also find yourself receiving a good many other callers – and a good deal of uninvited mail. If you put advertisements in newspapers carrying your home address then you may find that you soon will not have any privacy left at all. And remember that if your publishing business grows so too will the mail and the number of callers.

There are two main alternatives to using your home address.

The first, which is by far the most expensive, is to rent or buy an office. I do not suggest you do this until your publishing venture is an established success.

The second is to use some form of accommodation address. Your local Post Office will tell you how to rent a Post Office Box and this may, particularly to begin with, be the simplest and easiest solution. If you are expecting lots of different types of mail you can use more than one Post Office Box in order to help you differentiate between the types of mail.

27. HANDLING TELEPHONE CALLS

The telephone really becomes a problem when you start putting your telephone number on your advertisements. You should, therefore, think carefully before putting your home telephone number onto your advertisements. Do you really want people calling up 24 hours a day 7 days a week? The novelty might begin to fade after a week or two without sleep. You can, of course, have an additional line installed which you use exclusively for your publishing business. You can put a telephone answering machine onto the business line when you want to 'switch off'.

Alternatively, you can do what we do and hire an outside agency to handle your telephone calls at night, at weekends and on bank holidays. We pay them a fee and they collect together all our messages for us. This system works well.

28. Taking credit cards

To begin with you can run your small publishing business by taking cheques or cash. But, if your business grows as I hope it will, then you will eventually find that customers want to know if you will also take credit cards.

The big snag with taking credit cards is that it means dealing with banks and banks are, of course, full of people who wear suits and regard fun and humour with the same sense of distaste most people reserve for septic tanks. Naturally, the fact that you will be dealing with banks means that there will be lots of reasons for charging you fees. There will, of course, be a joining fee and every time you take a credit card order you will have to pay a small but noticeable percentage of the gross price to the credit card company. The credit card service charge is likely to be 3.5% to 4.0% though some cards charge an even higher percentage. There will, inevitably, be a minimum annual service charge requirement so don't even think about taking credit cards unless you think your business is likely to be big enough.

The big advantage of taking credit cards is that you will be able to take telephone orders for your books. Research by mail order companies has shown that advertisements do considerably better (and I really do mean considerably better) if customers can order by telephone as well as through the mail. Put a telephone number on an advertisement and tell your potential customers that you will accept payments by credit card and you could easily increase the number of orders you take by a half. That is enough to turn many loss making advertisements into profitable advertisements.

29. Dealing with queries

A surprisingly large amount of your time will be taken up with queries. Some of these will be serious, some will be trivial and some will be quite unbelievable. You will receive letters from people wanting you to publish their book. You will receive letters from people wanting you to give them copies of their book for free. (Unless you're in a good mood and feeling generous tell them that your book is available free of charge through every public library.) You will receive letters complaining about something you said or didn't say. You will receive letters offering you unique business opportunities. You may find that life will be easier if you have some cards or letters produced with little messages printed on them. You could either have several cards, all containing different messages, or one card with several messages listed – allowing you to tick the most appropriate response.

30. PACKING BOOKS

You can, if you like, try packing up books with brown paper, string and sealing wax. But I strongly recommend that you use padded bags of some kind. A padded bag will provide the protection your book needs to get it through the post safely. Make sure that you choose a light padded bag otherwise you will end up paying out a lot of extra money on postage. Books are heavy enough by themselves. You want your books to arrive at their destination in perfect condition but you also want the bag to be as light as possible.

When choosing a size for your book bear in mind the fact that it will have to fit inside a padded bag and be delivered through a normal letter-box. Check out the sizes of padded bags before insisting on having your book published in a very unusual size. If you can't pack and mail your oddly sized book without using cardboard, sealing wax and string you may regret your impetuosity and determination to be different.

31. INPUTTING ORDERS

If computers frighten you then you can, to begin with, keep your orders in a large notebook. You can use the same notebook to help you keep details of the money you have received. But if your business grows then you will obviously need to set up a program to keep details of your customers. You may, if you are clever with computers, be able to set up your own programme. But don't worry if you aren't clever with computers. You can always buy a purpose built mail order programme. The big advantage of a purpose built programme is that it will be ready programmed to give you much of, if not all, the information you are likely to need.

I would suggest that it is almost certainly worthwhile investing in a professionally produced programme. We at Publishing House have tried three software programmes. One was acceptable but slow and complicated. One was about as much use as a chocolate truncheon and had to be discarded (at enormous expense). The one we use at the moment makes life easier. It enables us to keep details of all our customers.

You will, of course, have to register your business under the Data Protection Act.

Whether you keep your customers names and addresses on bits of paper or in a computer make sure that you keep at least one constantly updated copy somewhere safe. If there is a fire you can replace equipment but your database of names and addresses is irreplaceable and potentially extremely valuable.

32. Keeping track of where the orders have come from

It is absolutely vital that you keep track of where your orders come from. You must know whether an advertisement or a mailshot has worked because if you don't then you may waste a great deal of money repeating an ineffective advertisement or lose a great deal of money by failing to repeat an effective advertisement.

If you use a computer then it isn't difficult to devise a simple spreadsheet to help you keep count of the orders received from individual advertisements. And by putting into the spreadsheet the cost of the advertisement and the cost of fulfilling those orders you can see at any instant (and at the end of every day) whether or not you are making a profit.

33. Keeping the accounts

If you are as hopeless as I am at doing accounts (I resent time spent poring over receipts and even the simplest accounts software package is a mystery to me) you may want to appoint an accountant if you don't already have one. I suggest that you ask around your friends to find an accountant who seems trustworthy, honest and reasonably priced. I dispensed with my accountant some time ago and don't use one at all but I do have someone at my office to prepare the figures for me.

You must remember that if your publishing venture does well and your turnover reaches a certain level (this varies from time to time according to the whims of the Chancellor of the Exchequer) you will have to register for Valued Added Tax (VAT). This isn't necessarily the disaster it might sound for when you are VAT registered you will be able to claim back the VAT you have paid on goods and services which you needed to be able to publish your book. At the time of writing there is no VAT on books themselves so you won't have to claim any VAT from the people who buy your books. Unless you have any other income which is liable to VAT (if, for example, you are paid for writing newspaper articles or columns or you have books which are published by conventional publishers) you may find that filling in the quarterly VAT form brings you a nice cheque from Her Majesty's Custom and Excise department.

34. Customer care

If you want your venture into publishing to succeed then you must look after your customers. Your aim should be not to think of ways to make life easier for *you* but to think of ways to make life easier and better for them. You want your customers to be satisfied so that they come back again and again and buy your books. You also want them to be so happy with the service you provide that they give your name to their friends. Providing a good service and a simple guarantee isn't enough. If you establish a good relationship with your customers then they will want you to grow and succeed (though not so much that you lose your friendliness and stop giving a good, personal service).

People want to be led but the rarest commodities in our world are honesty, respect and integrity and I believe that people do respect these old-fashioned virtues. The best way to grow stronger is to delight your customers so much that they help spread the word about your book(s) by word of mouth. Nothing sells books (or, indeed, anything else) as effective as word of mouth advertising.

Conventional publishers have one absolutely enormous drawback: their only contact with their customers is through a third party (the bookshops which sell their books). Naturally this makes it difficult for a conventional publisher to build up any sort of relationship with his customers. It is, indeed, virtually impossible for a publisher even to know who his customers are under those circumstances.

But since you will be selling most of your books by mail order you will have a huge advantage over them: you will, over the years, be able to compile a list of the people who have bought your books.

As I have suggested already, as soon as your business starts to make progress you should grit your teeth and invest in software that is suitable for someone running a mail order business. Alternatively, persuade a computer literate friend to write some special software for you. (If you are computer literate yourself you won't need the friend.)

Having the names and addresses of your customers on a computer database means that you can write to your customers on a regular (or irregular) basis to tell them about new books you are publishing or to offer them special deals on books that they already know about.

From time to time it is well worthwhile asking yourself why your current customers originally bought from you – and why they are likely to buy from you now. What are you good at? What is the undervalued (and possibly unstated) benefit to your customers of doing business with you?

For example, my monthly Health Letter is, superficially, a source of independent medical advice and information. But it is, I hope, a good deal more than that. I aim to remove some of the fear and anxiety that is these days associated with health and health care and to provide my readers with a companion who can guide them to a knowledge and understanding of better health and improved health care, an independence and ability to deal knowledgably with health care professionals (whether they be orthodox or complementary practitioners) and a feeling that they are not alone in a world where loneliness is endemic.

Are you doing everything you can to keep your customers happy – and to make sure that they continue to stay happy?

(Remember that customers who have returned books to you need not necessarily be lost for ever as future customers. Respond to their request for a refund quickly and politely. Apologise for the fact that the book they bought did not satisfy their expectations. Do not ask them to explain why they want a refund. Send them a catalogue with the refund cheque. You may want to include a discount voucher to encourage them to buy something else. Some publishers include a free gift with their refund cheque.)

Always remember that your customers are not buying books (or a newsletter) from you. They are buying entertainment, information or presents. And you must always 'sell' the benefit or else your customers won't realise how they benefit from their relationship with you.

The first sale of the first book should be the start of a relationship – not the end. You should always be looking for ways to improve life for the people who do business with you. Think of them as friends rather than as customers. I regard the people who buy my books and Health Letter as friends, and members of an extended family.

If, for any reason, you cannot deliver an ordered book within the promised time you should write and explain in honest, accurate detail what has gone wrong and why you cannot fulfil your promise. If a supplier has let you down then explain why and how – and describe what you normally do to make sure that this doesn't happen. If all your book stock has been destroyed in a fire then say so – and explain why and how the fire started and what you are doing about it. Remember how annoying it is when you are stuck on a train or at an airport and no one bothers to tell you why there is a delay. Finally, offer to send the reader his or her money back.

35. *Get the best out of your backlist – develop your own catalogue*

In the good old days publishers used to pay a great deal of attention to their backlist catalogue. A publisher's aim would be to find authors who would, over the years, write a number of steadily selling books. Promoting a new book by an author would, therefore, bring in new readers to buy and read his previous books. A good backlist catalogue could turn a marginally profitable publishing house into a relatively successful venture.

Most of today's modern, corporate publishers seem far too busy searching for this season's blockbuster success to take much interest in developing a good catalogue of backlist titles.

You, on the other hand, should take great care of your backlist. As you publish more and more new books you should take care to continue to sell the old books.

And automatically include a copy of your backlist catalogue with every book you send out.

When you have published two books you can put a catalogue or leaflet describing and advertising one of your publications whenever you sell the other. The more books you have on your backlist the more books you will be able to advertise when you send out books to your customers. Mailing promotional material in this way costs you hardly anything – just the cost of the leaflets and the cost of having someone stuff them into the envelopes. Unless you have a huge catalogue which weighs a great deal the chances are that your leaflet won't cost you anything in postage because it will be sent out free with a book you already have to post.

One of the big advantages you have over the conglomerates is that yours is a small and friendly business whereas they run large, impersonal empires. People tend to like small and friendly and dislike large and impersonal so use your advantage to the full. Printing in vast quantities means that they will be able to beat you on price but you can definitely beat them on service and quality.

You should always send out a short friendly note with every order (it doesn't have to be hand written or even signed) to thank the customer for ordering from you.

But there is something else important you can do to establish your friendly image. Once you have built up your publishing business large enough to need a catalogue you will probably have staff. Some of these may be friends or relatives just helping out part time. You can emphasise the friendliness of your publishing imprint by including a small section in your catalogue explaining who does what.

36. SELLING A BOOK IS THE BEGINNING NOT THE END

Selling a product or a service to a new customer should always be a beginning and not an end. It is in your interests to make sure that your customers know how to get the best out of whatever it is that you are selling.

If your business is not doing well then the chances are that you are either not providing what your customers (or potential customers) really want or that someone else is providing a better produce or service or the same product or service at a more competitive price.

Your customers should think of you as a friend.

You should work with and for your customers.

It is far more profitable in the long run. You may be able to make short term money by ripping people off. But if you want to create something worthwhile then you must encourage your customers to trust you. Provide good service (defined as high quality goods, provided in the right quantity and with a good spirit).

When things go wrong (as they assuredly will even though you may do your best to avoid and anticipate problems) apologise and put things right in a good spirit too. And if something does go badly wrong try to re-establish your fractured relationship with the customer by giving him or her a free gift. Try to deliver more than you promise. You should certainly never deliver less than you promise.

Remember that honesty and decency do lead to long term success – even though, in the short term, they may prove expensive and seem counter productive. People do respect honesty and integrity.

HOW TO BE A PUBLISHER – PART FOUR

HOW TO INCREASE YOUR PROFITS (AND MAKE EVEN MORE MONEY)

'No profit grows where is no pleasure taken.'   WILLIAM SHAKESPEARE

1. Never stop watching and learning

2. Serial rights

3. Foreign rights

4. Multimedia

5. The real truth about computers and the internet: profitable opportunities or expensive gimmicks?

6. Selling names and addresses

7. Export sales

8. Public lending right

9. Library suppliers

10. Promotional gifts

11. Start your own newsletter

HOW TO BE A PUBLISHER – PART FOUR

HOW TO INCREASE YOUR PROFITS AND MAKE EVEN MORE MONEY)

1. NEVER STOP WATCHING AND LEARNING

As your publishing business grows you should always be prepared to learn from others. Every time you meet or read about someone successful – whose work or life you admire – observe them and learn from what they do. Ask yourself what it is that they are trying to do (if you get the chance you could ask them). Find out their philosophies. Find out what drives them. And write down everything you learn. (Writing things down is the best way to remember them.)

Remember that every aspect of business life that can be measured can also be improved. And every aspect of business life (efficiency, sales per particular effort, profitability etc.) can be measured. You can only measure if you ask questions. And remember that you must ask the right questions. The quality of the questions you ask will have a fundamental effect on the quality of the answers you receive.

The single most important question in business (as in life) is: 'Why?'

The second most important question is: 'So what?'

Ask yourself these questions often.

Only by constantly questioning yourself and those who are working with you will you minimise your errors and improve your business.

At regular intervals you should assess your current marketing programmes. Ask yourself how much effort you are putting into each programme – and how much of your business comes from that programme. You may discover some surprising truths about your business. For example, you may find that you are putting a lot of effort into a marketing area which isn't really worthwhile.

You should ask yourself why people bought from you in the past and why they buy from you now. Ask yourself whether you are still offering as good a service as you used to offer. If you have lost some of your original hope, passion and ingenuity then maybe there is something you can do to regain those lost values.

At least once a year you should sit down and remember why you first started publishing your own books. You should ask yourself what you wanted to do. Try to decide if your aims have changed. And ask yourself how well you are satisfying those early targets.

You should ask yourself what you can offer readers that no one else can offer. What is your greatest advantage over your competitors? What is it about your business that makes you proudest? Are you proud of the books you are writing? Are you proud of how your books look? Are you proud of the service you are providing? (You should, of course, be able to answer 'yes' to all those questions.)

You should always be thinking of expanding your business – either by introducing new titles or finding new ways to sell the old ones. Keep looking and you will find new markets, new advertising opportunities and new ways to keep your backlist alive. You may, for example, find that a book which isn't selling as well as it used to sell might do better if you produce a new, more up to date edition, or if you used the same material to launch an audio cassette tape or a CD. The business which does not expand and grow and change and adapt will atrophy and die. There are four fundamental ways to expand a business.

First, you can find more customers. To do this you will have to make your product or service better known to a wider range of potential customers. You may be able to do this by advertising or by publicity or by encouraging your present customers to help you find new customers.

Second, you can encourage each customer to spend more money with you every time they buy (usually by buying more books).

Third, you can encourage your existing customers to come back to you more often.

And fourth, you can ask your customers to spread news about your book to their friends. Once your customers start telling their friends and relatives about your book then your business will boom.

Remember that the best way to grow is through word of mouth. Very large businesses know that however much money they spend promoting a new product (such as a new movie) the ultimate success or failure of the item will depend not upon the extent of the promotional expenditure but upon whether or not people like the product and recommend it to their friends.

But a warning: decide how big you want to be – and don't let your business get so big that it stops being fun. When you have more than one crisis a day you may have reached the point when it makes sense to cut back a little.

2. SERIAL RIGHTS

For reasons why I do not even begin to understand newspapers will pay far more when they are buying the right to serialise or take extracts from a book than they will if they are buying an article or a series of articles. They will pay thousands of pounds for an extract from a book when they would have probably paid only hundreds of pounds for an identical article.

I've sold serial rights in scores of books and I've written (literally) thousands of articles and columns for newspapers and magazines and I honestly have no idea at all why tough newspaper editors who will complain bitterly about a feature writer's £5 taxi bill on an expenses claim will happily authorise cheques for thousands of pounds (dollars or whatever) when bidding for the right to print something from a book.

A good friend of mine once wrote an article about the royal family. He then offered the article to a number of newspaper and magazine editors. One editor was mildly interested and offered £300 for the piece. The other editors either sent the article back or ignored it completely.

My friend (I'll call him Jack though that isn't his name) thought that the piece was worth considerably more than £300 but he wasn't exactly in a strong position. He either accepted the £300 he had been offered or kept the article and got absolutely nothing for it.

'Why don't you turn it into a book?' I asked him.

'A book!' said Jack, clearly horrified. 'I've never written a book. Besides the article is only 3,000 words long and I really don't think I could stretch it much further without more research. And I need money now.'

'You don't have to stretch it straight away,' I told him. 'But instead of offering it as an article offer it as an extract from a forthcoming book. Think up a sexy title, write a short foreword, an introduction and a contents list and call your 3,000 word article Chapter One. Then get someone with a colour printer to design and print out a dummy cover for you.'

'Once you've done that get a couple of dozen copies made, put them into folders and send them off to the editors who you think might be interested.'

Now, newspaper editors don't want to have to go to the trouble of reading a whole book. (To be perfectly honest, after working for just about every paper in what used to be Fleet Street, I'm not entirely sure that there are many newspaper editors around who actually could read a book.) They don't want to have to plough through several hundred pages of text in order to find a few thousand words they can use in their paper. They want to be presented with a nice, neat package ready for publication.

Jack followed my advice and sold his article (now redefined as a book extract) within five days. Three editors telephoned with offers and Jack finally did a deal for £8,500. Since he was selling an extract from a forthcoming book he sold only first British serial rights. Naturally, this meant that he could then also sell foreign rights to newspapers and magazines around the rest of the world.

Valuable Tips When Selling Serial Rights

1. When selling anything to a newspaper watch out for the infamous clause 'payable on publication'. Do not accept a contract or commissioning letter containing this phrase or anything like it. Your contract or letter should make it clear that the newspaper is agreeing to pay the sum agreed for whatever rights you are selling. If the phrase 'payable on publication' appears then you will not get paid if, for any reason, your book extract or article does not appear. Newspapers and magazines are notorious for buying material which they never use. The phrase 'payable on publication' gives them a wonderful let out and enables them to avoid paying you if a member of the royal family breaks a limb and all the commissioned material is suddenly thrown out of the paper. It is disappointing enough not to see your piece in print. Not getting paid makes the whole sorry business even more painful – particularly since it is extremely likely that the other editors who were interested in and excited by your book or article will, by now, have lost all interest in it. Newspaper editors have the attention span of five year old children and lose interest in features and stories very quickly.

2. I only ever sell local serial rights and you should too. Never, ever give copyright to a newspaper or magazine. Whether you are selling a book extract, serial rights, an article or a column you should only sell first local serial rights. If you are selling an article to a British paper then you should sell them First British Serial Rights. This gives the publication the 'first' right to publish the material. If you have already sold the article to one paper and you are now selling subsequent rights then these can be described as Second British Serial Rights, Third British Serial Rights and so on. Or you could simply sell the right to publish the material once. When you have sold your book about tennis to a national newspaper you can try selling additional rights to a specialist sports magazine.

3. Ask (or insist) that the editor put the words 'Copyright Vernon Coleman 2001' at the bottom of your article or book extract. If you don't want to give your copyright to me then you can insert your own name (and the correct year) in the appropriate places. If the article is taken from or is (however loosely) associated with a book you have written then make sure that you ask the editor to make sure that the copyright notice is accompanied by the name of your publishing house, the price and, if appropriate, the date of publication.

4. It is your responsibility to make sure that your article or book extract contains nothing libellous. In the good old days publishers and editors used to stand by their authors and writers. These days I am afraid that you have to assume that you are going to be on your own. If the paper which has published your work is sued then there is a good chance that they will do whatever protects their own interests while

throwing you to the dogs. It is not uncommon for newspapers to settle with people taking libel action against them. This can make it extremely difficult for the free-lance writer to formulate any sort of defence. Worse still, it is not unknown for a newspaper which has settled out of court to then demand that the writer pay their costs and whatever damages they paid.

5. Ask the editor to make sure that his newspaper's syndication department knows that the article is your copyright and that any enquiries from other editors wanting to publish your piece should be passed on to you.

6 If you are selling serial rights from a book which you have published you should ask the editor to allow you to sell your book 'off the page'. All this means is that at the bottom of the extract which appears in the paper something like this will appear: 'Readers can buy a copy of Vernon Coleman's book direct from the publishers and save £x off the published price. To obtain your copy send your name and address and a cheque or postal order for £y (cheques should be made payable to Publishing House) to: Vernon Coleman Book Offer, Publishing House, Trinity Place, Barnstaple, Devon EX32 9HJ.

3. FOREIGN RIGHTS

In an attempt to find an American distributor for our books I went to the London Book Fair. I also wanted to have a look around to see what the 'big boys' were doing. While I was there I was rather depressed. Everywhere I looked publishers seemed to be doing exactly the same things. There was a 'follow the leader' air to the whole dismal business. I remembered why I had lost faith and interest in traditional publishing companies, and had been happy to start publishing my own books.

When I left the book fair, which was held in Olympia, I walked back to Paddington Station to catch the train. By the time I reached the station I had cheered up. I had realised that the fact that most big publishing companies are still playing 'follow the leader' (without really knowing who the leader is, or where they are heading) was excellent news for a small, innovative and daring publishing company.

The fact is that there is a world-wide market for books which are different and which are written with passion. We have books on sale all around the world and rarely a week goes by without our receiving a letter, fax or telephone call from a foreign publisher wanting to publish one of our books.

The market for foreign rights is huge – and constantly growing. My books have sold in over 20 languages and in over 50 different countries around the world. Advances and royalties from some countries may be small – but all those $1,500 and $1,000 advances add up.

4. MULTIMEDIA

As a publisher you should be enormously grateful for the opportunities offered by 'multimedia'. Tapes, CDs and software have promised so much for so long that just about all the big publishers now spend a great deal of their time and money on attempting to market products in this area.

Sadly, for them but not for you and I, they have not found the multimedia explosion to be as profitable as it is fashionable. While the big publishing companies concentrate more and more of their money and energies on multimedia opportunities you and I can carry on with selling books and making a profit.

I have some personal experience of the multimedia fashion in publishing. I began selling computer software versions of my books back in 1981 and the remainder of the early 1980s. I remember producing a series of 'Home Doctor' cassettes back in the days when information was fed into computers by cassette. The 'Home Doctor' tapes and a computer version of my book *Aspirin or Ambulance* were sold in 26 countries and were, I believe, the world's first attempt at multimedia publishing.

There was, however, a rather large snag. We didn't make any money. I suspect that the explanation for this may simply have been that there weren't enough people with computers to make the software an attractive commercial proposition.

In the middle and late 1980s I started writing, recording and selling audio cassettes. There is quite a good market for these. Remember that VAT has to be added to the price of audio cassettes and CDs.

5. THE REAL TRUTH ABOUT COMPUTERS AND THE INTERNET: PROFITABLE OPPORTUNITIES OR EXPENSIVE GIMMICKS?

Back in 1995, when the internet first began to attract some attention, we arranged for a 36 page catalogue of our books to appear in an ethereal shopping arcade. We sold one book to a reader in Japan but although we posted the book we never received the money for it. I abandoned that whole venture quite early on.

Today, I still don't know of anyone (other than people in the computer business) who makes money out of the internet legally. (Though, having said that I do confess that one of our sites now does sell quite a few books and is profitable. But without the other facets of the publishing business the internet site would not work efficiently. The sales through other means keeps our book production costs down and helps keep office and fulfilment costs down too.)

The internet is a huge messy playground but as a selling medium it seems to me to be pretty damned useless. It is slow to use and the majority of sites are over laden with annoying advertisements. Much of the material on the internet is poorly designed and inefficient. It is poorly designed because the people designing it are computer nerds who understand nothing of people, business or, indeed, real life. (The advertisements are there because they are the only way the owners of many sites can bring in any money – but the advertising they carry on their sites doesn't bring in enough money to pay for the advertising the site owners buy in newspapers and magazines and on television.)

I doubt if there has ever been a more over-sold, over-hyped development in the history of the world. On each of the last three occasions when I tried to buy items using the internet I gave up in despair after spending an age waiting for things to happen. On each occasion I subsequently called directory enquiries, telephoned the relevant companies, gave my order and credit card number and completed the transaction in less time than it takes to log on to the internet.

If I want to do research it is still quicker (and more efficient) to pick a book off my shelves. It is also difficult to differentiate between those sites offering genuine, honest, information and those sites which have been set up solely to promote a particular commercial point of view. At the moment it is difficult not to compare the internet to the hula hoop, platform shoes, space hoppers and the mullet hairstyle: a fashionable accessory that may or may not have a real commercial future.

I am perfectly prepared to believe that the internet may become more useful in a few years time, and it will undoubtedly have a place to play in communication, education and business, (although for the dot companies to work they have to re-educate internet users – most of whom have grown accustomed to obtaining information and services without charge) but for the time being I am happy to concentrate most of my efforts on an apparently old-fashioned approach to publishing.

If you wish to play around with the internet for fun, or because you want to provide people with information, or because you have a hidden agenda which you wish to promote, then that's fine. But do not be misled into thinking that the internet offers a realistic route for the marketing and sale of books (or, indeed, anything else). A lot of technological development is needed before the internet will be a truly effective tool. And a lot of over-hyped dot com companies have to go bust before we can see the real strength of the internet.

***

As your publishing business grows so you will be told that you have to buy computers and software to help you keep track of your customers. It is true that computers can help you record your orders, keep a database of customers (don't forget that if you keep your customers' names on computer you have to satisfy privacy regulations under the Data Protection Act), and help you keep track of your finances. But try to remain cynical and sceptical. Don't allow yourself to be suckered into buying equipment or software which you don't really need and which isn't going to improve your life and/or make your business considerably more efficient and profitable. If a computer, or a piece of software, is worth buying then it should pay for itself within a year.

Remember that the computer industry seems to attract people who have a small, particular skill in one very specific area but whose level of general intelligence is pretty low. The support services provided are frequently expensive, difficult to reach and staffed by people who cannot communicate with callers because their standard of literacy is approximately the same as a teapot.

People in the computer industry provide an almost universally poor service; they are unreliable, snooty and either do not understand or do not care about the fears and needs of their customers. The average computer nerd is about as good as communicating with adults as is the average teenager. I thought that doctors were bad at talking to their patients but many of today's arrogant computer experts are infinitely worse. They are all medium and no message. (Many of them are also remarkably incompetent. It is commonplace to ring a computer company on six different occasions, speak to six different people and get conflicting advice on each occasion.)

You will probably suspect from this that I have had a number of unhappy experiences when dealing with computer hard and software suppliers. You are right. Who hasn't? But I have tried to ensure that my feelings on this matter are objective rather than subjective

***

How can you best survive in a world where computer technology (in its various forms) is now clearly here to stay? How can you minimise the amount of stress computers add to your life?

First, don't be afraid to ask yourself how a new piece of equipment is going to improve your life. If it isn't going to improve your life why are you buying it? If progress doesn't make your life better in some way then it isn't progress worth having. If a computer, or a piece of software, isn't going to pay for itself within twelve months then it isn't worth buying. Using a notebook and a pencil is still sometimes the best way to do things.

Second, always keep backups of your vital information. Computers (and allied accessories) break down regularly. The quality of workmanship (in both hardware and software) is poor. If you do not expect too much your disappointments will be fewer.

Third, don't trust anything anyone in the computer industry tells you. When they promise you backup they may be lying.

Fourth, don't be afraid to insist that the computer experts speak to you in a language you understand. Don't let them hide the fact that they are barely literate by confusing you with jargon.

Fifth, if you don't understand what something does, and how it is supposed to help you, don't buy it.

6. SELLING NAMES AND ADDRESSES

Once you have acquired a database containing a large number of names and addresses of customers, you can consider selling those names and addresses to other businesses who are in, or wish to enter, direct mail selling.

You can either do this yourself or via a list broker.

Some mail order companies make most of their money through selling names and addresses. We don't. We consider ourselves to be first and foremost a publishing house.

7. EXPORT SALES

At some point you may find yourself being contacted by a foreign distributor wanting to know if he can sell copies of your books in his country. This has happened to us quite frequently but only on one occasion has it proved profitable (and then the profit really only came through the fact that the increased sales enabled us to increase our print runs and therefore lower our production prices).

There are several snags with export sales.

The first is that you will almost inevitably be dealing with someone you have never met.

Second, is the fact that it is extremely expensive to send books long distances. Books are exceptionally heavy items but they are also easily damaged and so they have to be crated up and protected with vast quantities of bubble wrap or something similar.

The third problem is the fact that you will have to fill in so much damned paperwork to move books out of your country and into his country that you will begin to wonder whether the whole exercise is worthwhile.

Fourth, comes the fact that you will, of course, probably be paid in a foreign currency. You will, therefore, have to make an allowance for the currency risk. Naturally, a whole series of banks will want to share in your good fortune in selling your books abroad. Banks may well be the only people to benefit from your efforts. Indeed, it is possible that your best chance of profiting from exporting your books will be to buy bank shares.

The fifth problem is the fact that all these problems will mean that your books will almost certainly have to be priced at a higher level than the local market can bear. In the US books are very cheap and imports usually seem horrendously expensive.

The sixth problem is the fact that you may have a considerable amount of difficulty in persuading your foreign distributor to send you any money. This problem can usually be avoided by insisting that they send you money before you send them books. Distributors who refuse to do this can safely be avoided on the grounds that they would have probably never come up with the money anyway.

The best solution for everyone is to try and sell reprint rights rather than trying to export copies of books.

8. Public lending right

As an author you are entitled to a small income calculated according to the number of times your book is borrowed from public libraries. This money comes directly from the government and so you should take every penny you are entitled to. (You will, of course, pay tax on it in due course so the government will get some of its own money back.)

The annual cheque from the Public Lending Right Office is extremely welcome but it is also good to receive a printout from the PLR office showing how many people have borrowed your books from public libraries.

To avoid spending too much of the available money on administration a small group of public libraries is used to check on library usage and your cheque is then calculated by adjusting this figure for the national number of libraries.

9. Library suppliers

A few years ago library suppliers were extremely important for all publishers: they would buy stocks of most books being printed and then distribute those books to libraries around the country. Cutbacks in library budgets has meant that this valuable source of income has more or less been lost. It is not unreasonable to expect to sell some books to libraries but your sales through this route will probably be modest.

10. Promotional gifts

Many publishers make a good deal of their income by selling their books to companies who want 'give aways' for their customers. For example, if you publish a book about Paris or about France you might be able to persuade a travel company, a villa rental company, a credit card company or some other organisation to buy copies from you to give away. If you do this the chances are that you will have to discount the book heavily. The advantage to you is that if you can arrange the sale before you finalise your print order you will be able to print more copies and therefore bring down your unit print costs.

11. START YOUR OWN NEWSLETTER

Most people in newspaper, magazine and book publishing turn up their noses at newsletter publishing. They think it is a fringe activity. They regard it as something people do for a hobby.

Here's some information to help you decide whether newsletter publishing is worthwhile:

❖ I know of one newsletter in the US which sells over 500,000 copies a year. Each subscriber pays around £37.

❖ I know of another newsletter with 5,000 subscribers – each paying around £250 a year.

Assume that it costs a maximum of £12 a year to print and send out monthly newsletters to a single subscriber (and remember that production and postage costs go down as the circulation increases) then work out the profits the publishers of these two newsletters are making.

Newsletter publishing is a fringe activity? Really? A hobby? Some hobby!

If you have an expertise which you are prepared to share with others then you can write, publish and sell your own regular newsletter.

Publishing House produces and distributes *Dr Vernon Coleman's Health Letter* every month. Within two years our newsletter had readers in 17 different countries.

How do you choose a topic for a newsletter?

Easy.

What are you interested in? What specialist knowledge do you have – or could you obtain?

If you've already published a book then the subject of your book is probably a good topic for your first newsletter. You'll have a good deal of information – and you'll know where to get more. As the author/publisher of a book on the subject you are now an 'expert'. And you can promote and sell your newsletter to the people who have bought your book – or who buy it in the future.

If you're interested in breeding dogs you could produce a newsletter on dog breeding. There must be thousands of other individuals out there who are desperate for information. If your hobby is photography why not produce a newsletter for amateur photographers? Give them tips, information on new equipment and suggest places where they can get their photographs published. If you are left-handed and play golf turn your knowledge into money by starting a newsletter for left-handed golfers. If you are female, left-handed and play golf why not start a newsletter for female, left-handed golfers?

There is almost no group of people too small to merit a newsletter. Big magazine publishers won't cater for left-handed golfers because there aren't enough of them but as a newsletter publisher you can concentrate on small specialist groups. Maybe there are only 1,000 female left-handed golfers willing to pay for information, tips and news. But wouldn't you be willing to make them all happy for £37 a year each?

If you don't think you can write and edit your own newsletter find a writer to do that part of the work for you. And either pay him or her a fee or a percentage of the profits. You won't have difficulty in finding a writer prepared to take on this work. If you don't know anyone suitable simply put a small advertisement in your local newspaper or in a suitable specialist magazine. For example, if you are looking for a writer to write and edit a newsletter on stamp collecting advertise in a stamp collectors' magazine.

Printing? That's easy too. Simply find a local printer and negotiate a price for your publication. You don't need anything fancy so don't spend a fortune on glossy paper or expensive colour printing. Remember: you are selling information. The presentation really doesn't matter all that much. It's the message not the medium that people will buy. Some of the biggest and most successful newsletters in the world look as though they have been printed in a back bedroom by a novice. It's done deliberately, to make the subscriber feel that he's buying something special – almost personalised – rather than something manufactured for the mass market. Remember that corporate newsletters which are printed on expensive art paper and which are full of photographs of the managing director are usually dumped straight into the bin. It's what you put into your newsletter that counts. Not what it looks like.

Where do you find the subscribers for your newsletter?

The easiest way is to send promotional material to the people who have bought your book(s). You can keep costs to an absolute minimum by enclosing a leaflet for your newsletter with every book you send out. As you acquire subscribers compile a list of quotes from their letters. Print the quotes on a leaflet to include in with your promotional material. This leaflet will help 'sell' your newsletter to new subscribers.

You can put flyers advertising your newsletter in magazines and newspapers or you can post your leaflet direct to potential subscribers whose names and addresses you have bought from another publisher.

Once you have set up your newsletter, and built up the circulation to a reasonable figure, you can include flyers advertising your own products. When you publish a new book on a subject which might interest your subscribers put a flyer advertising the book in with your newsletter.

And you can allow outsiders to include their leaflets in with your newsletter – for a fee, of course. They pay for the printing of their own leaflets and you put the leaflets in your newsletter. But watch out: if the weight of their promotional literature is too high your newsletter may move into another posting band – and you could lose all the money you've made from them.

Finally, don't forget that once you have set up your newsletter publishing operation there is nothing at all to stop you starting a second newsletter. Then a third and a fourth...

AFTERWORD

You will find that becoming a publisher will give you more freedom, more independence and more power than virtually anything else you can do. Being a publisher gives you a voice – a small voice, perhaps, but nevertheless a voice. To begin with you can just reach out to a handful of people. Then, as you become more successful, you will find that your message reaches hundreds, thousands and, in the end, possibly even millions of other people.

One final piece of advice. Grow at your own pace. Grow your business at a rate you feel comfortable with. At Publishing House we have, so far, sold nearly 400,000 books – and countless reports, tapes and other publications. At times we have been tempted to expand too quickly. That can create problems. For example, the bigger you become the more staff problems you will have. Endless supplies of new legislation mean that managing a business which grows too quickly, or too far, can turn a pleasure into a burden.

But, that's a good problem to have.

I wish you good luck with your publishing venture.

There are only three reasons to do something: to change the world, to have fun and to make money. Publishing will enable you to do all three of those things at once.

Vernon Coleman, Devon 2001

GLOSSARY OF PUBLISHING AND PRINTING TERMS

Advance Information Sheet

Promotional sheet describing a forthcoming book. Contains brief details of the book (author, publisher, price and a short resumé of the contents). A.I. sheets are posted to bookshops and others likely to buy the book.

Back end sales

A sale made to a customer who has already bought a book from you. Most of the real profits to be made out of mail order publishing are made through 'back end sales'.

Backlist

Previously published books which are still in print and therefore still available. Many orthodox, traditional publishers pay remarkably little attention to their backlist titles and ignore the opportunity for long term, steady sales – and a long term, steady income.

Bar code

A code which contains the ISBN and the selling price of the book which is printed on the back cover of the book and makes a mess of the design. Bar codes can be read by machines but not by humans unless they are very, very clever and yet such miserable human beings that they have nothing better to do than learn how to read them.

Bleed

A printing term. When whatever is printed on a page runs right up to the very edge of the paper it is said to bleed.

Blurb

Information found on book covers and jackets (as well as advertisements) which describe the contents of the book – and usually include something about the author too.

Body copy

The main text within an advertisement.

Book

According to UNESCO a book is a non periodical publication which contains 49 or more pages, excluding the cover.

Book fair

Places (often abroad and most notably in Frankfurt, Germany) where self important people who know very little about anything and much less about books rush around looking extremely important and selling each other rights in books none of them have read.

Bromide

A photographic image of artwork to be used in a book, catalogue or advertisement.

Buyer

Person in a bookshop who has the responsibility for selecting and ordering books for stock. (Alternatively, a sensible, thoughtful, well read, sophisticated individual who hands over money in exchange for one of my or your books).

Camera ready copy

Typeset text which is ready to be photographed to make the litho plate ready for printing.

Carriage

Shipping books from somewhere to somewhere. As the publisher you will almost certainly be responsible for carriage costs.

Carriage – forward

The bookseller chooses how to have the book delivered to him. And he pays the carriage costs. You will not be surprised that this is a rare method of moving books from publisher to bookseller.

Carriage – free

The publisher pays for the delivery to the bookshop. And, as a reward for paying, the publisher can choose the route (e.g. through the Post Office or a carrier).

Case bound

A hardback book.

Chain bookshop

A bookshop that belongs to a chain of stores.

Character

A space, letter, symbol or punctuation mark.

Charter bookshop

Alleged to be a rather superior sort of bookshop with a good variety of stock.

Closed market

If you sell Russian rights in a book to a Russian publisher and no one else can publish that book in Russia then Russia becomes a closed market as far as that book is concerned.

Colophon

A publisher's logo. Makes the publisher feel important but is a waste of time and money and is unlikely to sell you any more books. (How many books do you buy because you like the colophon?)

Commission

A percentage of the money brought in by an agent and paid to him as a reward for his services.

Copy

Words.

Copyright

The exclusive right to material (usually written). Copyright belongs to an author unless he has specifically sold it to someone else. No author should ever, ever sell his copyright in a piece of work. He should lease it or sell the right to use his work, or at most, assign part of the copyright.

Counter pack

A special container which is sent to bookshops in the hope that they will use it to display copies of your book. Ideally a counter pack should sit next to the till so that customers see it at their most vulnerable (when they have their wallets or purses open). Bookshops receive so many counter packs that yours is likely to be thrown straight into the bin.

Credit note

Someone owes someone money but doesn't want to part with hard cash. If you owe a bookseller money (because he has returned books to you and doesn't want to buy anything else you have for sale) then you can give him a credit note instead of sending him a cheque. He will be thrilled by this.

Database

Information kept in a computer file. Your most important database will be the list of names and addresses of your customers. If you keep this on a computer then you should keep several copies (regularly updated) in safe places.

Delivery note

A note sent with books sent out to a publisher. Usually this will be a copy of the invoice and will detail the books being sent, the discounts and the prices owed.

Desk Top Publishing

A computer, some software and a printer. You can publish commercially using DTP as long as you hire a real printer to produce your books. If you use your own home printer then whatever you produce will always look rather amateurish. Sorry.

Direct costs

The costs that can be related specifically to one book. Direct costs include printing and binding costs, for example.

Discount

The amount the publisher knocks off the retail price when selling to a bookshop or wholesaler or good customer or anyone prepared to hand over hard cash.

Distributor

Organisation which stocks books and supplies them to bookshops. You can hire a professional distributor to warehouse your books and send them out to bookshops and members of the public. They will charge you a fee for every book they send out and you will have to send them all the instructions. There is, inevitably, a good chance that things will go wrong. If you want to save money and have the space to store your own books you can handle your distribution yourself.

Dues

Orders bookshops place with a publisher for books which are not yet available – either because they have not yet been printed or because they are being reprinted.

Dump bin

A large free-standing cardboard container which occupies a good deal of floor space in a bookshop and sells the books of a single author or publisher. You can have dump bins made if you like but they will probably end up being dumped in the bin.

Edition

An edition of a book includes all the copies which are printed without any significant changes to the text. One edition may, therefore, include several impressions or printings.

Electronic stock control (EPOS)

A cashier wipes a special pen over the barcode and a computer somewhere takes note. Electronic stock control enables bookshop buyers to see which books are selling and which are not – it makes it easier for bookshops to return books to the publisher.

Em

The amount of space occupied by the letter 'm' in your chosen typeface and point size. The letter 'm' is chosen because it is the widest letter in the alphabet.

Embargo

If you have a red hot press release and you want to stop editors using it before a certain time then you can put an 'embargo' on it. Theoretically, this will protect your information and make sure that one newspaper doesn't use the story as an exclusive – thereby stopping other newspapers from running the story. Sadly, editors tend not to take much notice of press embargoes these days. Publishers used to put embargoes on books sent out for review but this is rather a waste of time these days since literary editors, being an unusually low lot, no longer take any notice of such things.

Estimate

A guess at the cost of a project. Printers' estimates are probably slightly more reliable than builders' estimates.

Firm sale

This is what every publisher wants to hear. It means that a bookseller who is ordering books isn't going to want to send them back. He is buying them 'firm sale' and agreeing to keep them even if he can't sell them. (When a small publisher sells books 'firm sale' it usually either means that the bookseller already has customers for the books or that the publisher is giving a massive discount.)

Format

The shape and size of a publication. The format also includes the number of pages and the type of binding.

Fulfilment

Receiving, processing and dispatching orders from customers.

Gross profit

The total value of book sales minus major overheads such as printing. Overhead costs are not taken out of gross profit. When overhead costs are removed you are (hopefully) left with net profit.

Imposition

An arrangement of all the pages of a book, in the correct order and ready for printing.

Impression

All the copies of a book which are printed at one time without the printing plates being altered.

Imprint

The number under which a publishing house issues its books. At Publishing House we have three imprints: European Medical Journal (EMJ), Chilton Designs and Blue Books. We use the EMJ for books on health and medicine, CD for fiction and Blue Books for everything else.

Indirect costs

Costs which cannot be related directly to a specific title. Telephone and heating costs are indirect. (Of course if you only have one title then all your costs could reasonably be described as 'direct'.)

In house

Work done by a publisher – as opposed to work which is put out to an outside organisation. So, if you are designing a book cover yourself you could describe this task as being kept 'in house'.

Insert

A promotional leaflet inserted into a periodical. It usually stays there until the periodical is placed on the newsagent's shelf when it falls onto the floor.

Invoice value

The amount shown on an invoice. This will usually be the retail value of the books, minus the discount agreed with or generously given to the bookseller or wholesaler.

ISBN

Stands for International Standard Book Number. Every book has a ten digit number these days. The ISBN helps to identify a book if it gets lost a long way from home. The first group of numbers may tell you the country of origin. The second group of numbers allegedly defines the publisher. The third group apparently describes the book (including the edition and whether it is hardback or paperback). And the fourth group is said to be a check on all the others.

ISSN

An eight figure identification number given to a periodical. The letters ISSN stand for International Standard Serial Number.

Landscape

The shape of a publication or photograph when the width exceeds the height.

Library supplier

Rather surprisingly, a firm which specialises in supplying books to libraries.

Limp

Paradoxically this term is usually used to describe a paperback which has pretensions and, because it is made with a slightly better cover, is a sort of half way house between a paperback and a hard back.

List

The titles a publisher has for sale. Our list include all the books published under our three imprints. If you are publishing just one book to start with then your list will be very short but it will still be a list.

List broker
A company or individual who sells mailing lists of names and addresses to companies or individuals who want to send out a direct mail promotion.

Mailshot
When promotional leaflets are sent out to potential book buyers.

Marketing
All those activities which are designed to ensure that a book is bought by as many people as possible. Your sales, distribution, advertising and promotional departments (probably all you when you begin) will be gathered together under 'marketing'.

Mark up (1)
Preparing a manuscript for the typesetter by scribbling little messages all over it.

Mark up (2)
Pushing up the price of a book because you realise that you have screwed up and forgotten to include some costs when working out your publication price. Marking up your price may then enable you to discount the price.

Media buyer
A professional who earns a living buying advertising space for clients. The media buyer makes his money from commissions paid by the magazines and newspapers in which his clients buy space.

Minimum order
Large, snotty publishers will sometimes only deal with a bookshop if they send a 'minimum order' (e.g. for 10 or 20 books). Publishing House has a minimum order of one. We are not too proud or important to sell books one at a time.

Net profit
Anything left over after all the costs of production and the overheads have been deducted. Large publishing companies don't usually have to worry about this because they don't make any profit. Hopefully, you will.

Net receipts
The amount of money a publisher receives after the cost of postage or carriage has been deducted.

Not Yet Published
If you get bookshop orders for a book that you haven't yet published you write NYP on the order and send it back.

On consignment

Some publishers are so utterly desperate to sell their books that they will let the bookshops have them for free (on consignment) trusting that if any books are sold they will eventually be paid for them.

On costs

General costs (heat, light etc.) that are shared between all the books being published by one publisher.

Open market

Part of the world where there is a free for all and anyone can sell a book – in whatever edition they like.

Origination

The various stages involved in preparing a manuscript for the printer. This may include editing, setting and providing the illustrations.

Orphan

The first line of a paragraph which is the last line on a page. Considered rather ungainly. You can usually get rid of an orphan by stretching the copy above and creating one more line.

Out of print (O/P)

Very sad news for the pessimistic author. But, good news for an optimistic author who sees an opportunity to sell the rights to another publisher or to bring out a new edition by himself.

Out of stock (O/S)

The book isn't currently available but will be reprinted and therefore available before the end of the next millennium.

Overheads

Salaries, office expenses and other general costs that do not relate to a specific book.

Page

One side of a piece of paper in a book is a page. Both sides of the same piece of paper are a leaf. Two pages side by side are a double page spread.

Pamphlet

According to UNESCO a pamphlet contains less than 49 but more than 8 pages. (Below 8 pages it is presumably a leaflet).

Perfect binding

Doesn't refer to the quality of the binding but to the fact that the back bits of the various signatures of the book are trimmed and then glued to the inside of the cover. Perfect binding is more expensive than simply stapling the pages together but cheaper than sewing. If you bend back a perfectly bound book you may crack it and if you do the pages will then all fall out.

Point of sale

Promotional material designed to be displayed in bookshops in order to try to sell books. Usually kept in a back room where it won't get in the way of customers.

Portrait

The shape of a publication or photograph when the height exceeds the width.

Postlims

Printed pages that come at the end of the book, using up pages that would otherwise be blank and therefore a waste of paper. Many large, snooty publishers leave these pages blank. We always put advertisements for our books on the postlim pages.

Prelims

The pages of a book that precede the real stuff. Like the short travelogues and news items that used to be shown in the cinema. Prelims can be paginated in roman numerals to show that the book hasn't really started yet and that the publisher knows about roman numerals.

Press release

A document sent out by publishers and thrown away by journalists.

Print run

The number of copies of a book published in one go.

Production ledger

Big publishers keep a record of all the expenditure incurred by a particular title – and then check this against their estimates. This is, however, exceedingly boring and so we don't bother.

Pro forma invoice

An invoice that must be paid before the publisher will part with the book or books. If you aren't sure that the bookseller will pay you then send him a pro forma invoice.

Promotion

Advertising and publicity designed to sell more books.

Proofs

A sign that something is happening and that the printer hasn't forgotten about your book. You will save a great deal of money if you do all your planned corrections before your book goes to the printer. Just remember that when the printer starts work every new comma or corrected error will cost you money.

Publication date

Moveable feast. The official date on which the book will go on sale to the public. Newspapers and other periodicals are not officially allowed to review a book before publication date. No one takes any notice of publication dates. Bookshops sell books when they get them and periodicals review them when they have the space. A publication date does, however, give a publisher and an author (in my and your case the same person) a chance to have a good meal and celebrate. You can alter the publication date if you need to fit in with a magazine schedule and they say that they will not run an extract or a review if they are going to be too far after your publication date. Don't tell anyone but some of our books have several publication dates.

Published price

List price – or the price at which a book is due to be sold.

Rate Card

The price at which publishers like to sell advertising space in their publications. No self respecting publisher should pay rate card unless he is deliberately trying to go bankrupt as quickly as possible.

Reading

A rather sad occasion when an author reads bits of his book out loud to a small group of very loyal readers, the vast majority of whom could just as easily read the book for themselves.

Recto

Right hand page. (The front of a leaf.)

Remainders

Books sold off cheap because they can't be sold at their proper price. Remainder merchants will often pay pitiful, knock down prices for the books they buy (often only a tiny fraction of the print costs). However, some remainder merchants do pay more reasonable prices for the books they buy and it is not unknown for large publishers to deliberately publish books to sell in remainder shops and on the remainder tables of bookshops. I was shocked to the core when I heard that this happened.

Reprint

A cause for celebration. Printing a second, third, fourth or even later impression of a book. If you want to tell a bookshop that a book is reprinting you can use the abbreviation R/P.

Review copy

Book sent out to newspapers or magazines. They will probably sell it to a friendly bookshop. They will probably not review it.

Review slip

A small piece of paper containing details of the book being sent for review and asking the literary editor to send a copy of any review published. Pitiful really, isn't it?

Rights

Every book has all sorts of rights. Paperback rights. Korean hardback rights. Portuguese book club rights. Film rights. Television rights. Radio rights. And so on. Successful, profitable publishing depends upon selling lots of rights.

Royalty

The percentage of the list price paid over to the author by a publisher.

Sale or return

The bookseller takes books, keeps them until they get battered and grubby and then sends them back to the publisher who throws them away. The sale or return policy is one of the main reasons why big publishers don't make any money. When booksellers return books to big publishers they will usually accept payment as an extension of their credit. (In other words they send back one book they can't sell and, in exchange, receive a similarly valued supply of another book they probably won't be able to sell.) When booksellers return a book to a small publisher they will usually demand a refund in cash – arguing that there isn't anything else on the list that they want to stock. Demands for cash refunds should be strongly resisted.

Sans serif type

A typeface which has no sort of twiddly stroke thing at the end of the line of a character.

See safe

Books sent to a bookshop on the agreement that they may be returned for credit or for a supply of another book if they do not sell.

Self ends

Printing term used to describe what happens when the first and last pages of the book are glued down to make the inside of the cover.

Serif

Type with a sort of twiddly thing at the end of every line of each character.

Short term

Advertising space which is left over and sold off cheaply close to the moment when the presses start to roll.

Signature

A folded sheet of printing, usually containing 16 or 32 pages. Books are made up of signatures and are, therefore, usually comprised of chunks of 16 or 32 pages.

Signing session

Very sad occasion when an author arrives at a bookshop and the staff and their relatives rush round and round in circles giving him books to sign because no one has turned up.

Single copy

Sale of one copy of a book. (Publishers like to make up jargon.)

Sleeper (1)

A book that doesn't sell very quickly to start with but eventually sells well. If your book is a disaster you can always say that it is an incipient sleeper.

Sleeper (2)

A name put into a mailing list so that the person selling the mailing list can tell if the list has been used more than once. (Or more times than have been paid for.)

Solus position

When there is just one advertisement on a whole page in a newspaper or magazine.

Specifications

The details of a book sent to a printer to get a quote. (Giving the number of pages, format, type of paper, binding etc.)

Spinner

Revolting display unit used in bookshops to display books. Alternatively a folk singer.

Subscription orders

Pre-publication orders for a book.

Teleordering

Clever electronic system enabling booksellers to send book orders to publishers via a central clearing house system.

Terms

The discount and the credit period offered by a publisher to a bookseller.

Title

In addition to the name of a book the word 'title' is sometimes used to denote all the books with that publisher. So a publisher may say: 'We have six new titles coming out this year.'

Trade sales

Books sold through bookshops as opposed to books sold through greengrocers.

Turnover

The total value of books sold within a specific period (usually a year).

Unit cost

The cost of producing all the copies of a single title divided by the number of copies printed. So if you have 1,000 books printed at a cost of £9,000 the unit cost is £9 and you are probably in big trouble.

Verso

A left hand page. The back of a leaf.

Wholesaler

Someone or a company who buys books in bulk from a publisher and then sells them onto bookshops and other retailers.

Widow

A single line or, worse still, a single word at the top of a page. Doesn't look nice but can usually be eradicated by fiddling with the text on the same or the previous page. Getting rid of a widow on one page usually creates an orphan (q.v.) or a widow on another page.

For a catalogue of Vernon Coleman's books please write to:

Publishing House • Trinity Place • Barnstaple • Devon EX32 9HJ • England

Telephone: 01271 328892 • Fax: 01271 328768

Outside the UK:
Telephone: +44 1271 328892 • Fax: +44 1271 328768

Or visit our websites:

www.vernoncoleman.com
www.lookingforapresent.com
www.makeyourselfbetter.net
